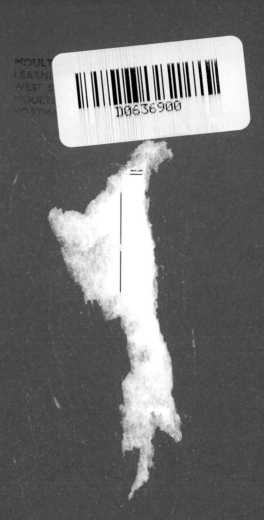

All-Weather Surfaces for Horses

Ray Lodge
and Susan Shanks

J.A. ALLEN · LONDON

© Ray Lodge and Susan Shanks 1994, 1999, 2005
First published in Great Britain by J. A. Allen in 1994
Revised edition 1999
Third edition 2005

ISBN 0 85131 913 0

J. A. Allen
Clerkenwell House
Clerkenwell Green
London ECIR OHT

J. A. Allen is an imprint of Robert Hale Limited

The production and use of fibred rubber and rubber products as referred to in this
book is protected by the brand name SPRINGWAY ® and patent GB 2244988
The SPRINGWAY Conduit Base System is protected by patent GB 2327585

A catalogue record for this book is available from the British Library

Design by Paul Saunders
Edited by Martin Diggle
Line illustrations by Hugo Shanks

All text photographs by the authors except for the photographs of Horse Guards
Parade and arena polo, reproduced by permission of Parkway Arenas and the
photograph of polo on Smith's Lawn, supplied courtesy of Guard's Polo and
© Centaur Photographic

Colour separation by Tenon & Polert Colour Scanning Limited, Hong Kong
Printed by New Era Printing Co. Limited, Hong Kong

Dedicated to Pat, and for P. J. D., C. D. and H. C. S.

Contents

List of Illustrations and Photographs   9

Introduction   11

1 Our Own Process of Discovery   15

2 The Aim of an All-weather Surface   21

3 General Principles of Construction   23
The Site
Size and Surface Material
The Base
Cost

4 Project Responsibility   27

5 Site Selection and Survey   29

6 Choice of Surface   31
Drainage Properties of Surfaces
Sourcing Surface Materials

7 The Base   38
Water Run-off and Conservation
Our Own Development

8 Material Migration   49

9 Maintenance Procedures   52

10 Maintenance Equipment   55

11   Why and When an Arena Fails   58

12   Construction Alternatives – an Overview   60
Sand
Wood
Plastic- and Rubber-based Surfaces
Sand bonded with Monofilament Fibre
Oil-bound and Wax-bound Surfaces

13   Summary of Arena Selection Procedure   70

14   The Value and Construction of Lunge Arenas   74

15   Construction of Gallops and Racecourses   76

16   Racecourse Surfaces – the Past and Future   80
The Position to Date
Future Possibilities

17   Indoor Surfaces   86

18   Health, Safety and Environmental Issues   89
Waste Rubber from Tyres
Oils and Preservatives
Water Conservation
General Safety

19   A New Project: Reinforced Turf   92
Early Equestrian Experiments
Other Experiments and Uses
The Position at Present

20   The Way Forward – a Future for Equestrian Sport   101
Racing
Eventing
Other Disciplines
County Shows

Index   109

List of Illustrations and Photographs

Illustrations

Cross-sections through typical arenas	38
Ground preparation for the arena on a sloping site	39
Cross-section through a sealed base arena	40
The jar test	50
Cross-section through The Severals track	78

Photographs

Our original all-weather arena at Village Farm	17
The Severals warm-up track at Newmarket	30
The range of sands and grits that can be used	32
Close-up of a wood fibre surface	32
PVC granules recovered from cable	33
Waste material from mouldings	34
Fibred rubber recovered from tyres	34
The experimental base system	43
The base	43
Pre-mixing the surface	43
Laying the surface	43
Construction of the international dressage arena	45
Site preparation – the plastic liner being laid	45
Conduits installed and concrete base laid	45
The elephant pump	46
The curb being laid	46
The premixed surface being laid	47
The clean pond that was incorporated into the system	47
The first test ride	48
The finished arena	48
Premixed fibre rubber surface, rolled to provide a good surface with minimal kick-back	53
Tractor-mounted maintenance roller	56
Simple, low-cost maintenance system	56
A typical all-weather dressage arena	62

The all-weather showjumping arena at Carluke   62
A fibred rubber and grit sand arena   65
Fibred rubber and grit sand in close up   66
Sand and waste material bonded with wax   68
Horse Guards Parade: Eurotrack surface on asphalt base   68
Acceptable 'kick-back': below knee height and not dusty   77
A fibred rubber gallop being test-ridden for the Jockey Club   77
Reinforced turf showing resistance to poaching   84
Portable arena for BETA 1997   87
A purpose-laid *Springway Fibre* riding-in track around an all-
    weather arena   93
A cross-country practice fence at Brockenhurst, sited on an
    'above ground' all-weather surface   94
Lucinda Green taking a jump with an all-weather landing area
    at Rademon   95
All-weather take-off and landing areas at the Irish National
    Championships   95
Poached ground after dressing with *Springway Fibre*/sand mix   96
Regenerated grass   97
Turf growing through *Springway Fibre*   98
A *Springway Fibre* gallop   98
Shows often have to cope with poor weather conditions   99
Reinforced turf withstands the passage of Shire horses and drays   100
A traditional point-to-point course   102
Practice arena at Burghley: a *Springway* reinforced turf surface   103
Arena polo on a Eurotrack wax-bound surface   104
Springway Fibre being sprayed over the Guards' polo ground,
    Smith's Lawn, Windsor   105
Smith's Lawn after spraying with *Springway Fibre*   106
The Royal Enclosure at Smith's Lawn after turf reinforcement
    and reseeding   106
Polo action on the reinforced surface at Smith's Lawn   107

Introduction

THIS BOOK IS NOW in its third edition. When the first edition was published in 1994, our Introduction read as follows:

The purpose of this book is to provide information about artificial riding surfaces. Although 'all-weather' has become the accepted term used to describe artificial surfaces, few are genuinely usable in all weathers. In some cases this is because they are basically unsuitable but, in others, availability could be improved by appropriate maintenance procedures.

Our experience of dealing with trade enquiries indicates that many people do not have enough information regarding types of surfaces available, their properties and maintenance requirements. We believe it is necessary to design and cost the complete installation and to establish maintenance requirements and costs over a given period before commencing a project to install an all-weather surface, be it a manège, showjumping arena, gallop or racetrack.

In many situations, provision of all-weather surfacing is essential in order to derive maximum pleasure from the horse, while ensuring the horse's well-being. Therefore, optimum selection of surface to meet a specific need is necessary. We hope that the information provided in this book will assist in such selection.

The crux of what we wrote then remains true today – the main aim of our book is to provide readers with comprehensive information about the various materials and methods that can be used in the construction of artificial riding surfaces. However, as we noted in the Introduction to the second edition, published in 1999, experience brings new developments and external factors combine to bring changes in the price and availability of raw materials. That was certainly true of the five-year period from 1994–1999, and it is probably the case that the subsequent years have seen changes with a greater net effect. Thus, while we have revised this new edition to keep readers up to date with recent developments, it may be true to say that, in addition to remaining a comprehensive guide, this book also, in some respects, offers a history of arena construction.

While the factors that have recently impacted on construction are detailed as appropriate within the chapters of this book, a brief summary of key points arising since publication of the second edition may be helpful. These are:

- Protection of the environment has become a major factor in arena construction. Legislation now requires installers and operators of sports surfaces to demonstrate that water discharged into drainage systems does not contaminate water supplies.

- In addition to avoiding water contamination, water conservation is becoming an important issue, since demand is exceeding supply. These issues, in combination, have an impact on the construction of arena bases and drainage systems.

- One spin-off of the legislation designed to avoid water contamination is that it has become difficult to find clean sands, as washing silt into rivers is no longer permitted. Further to this, a tax on aggregates means that both sand and quarry stone are now expensive commodities.

- There has been a significant ebb and flow in the availability of suitable rubber material available from used tyres. With the introduction of wire-reinforced car tyres, the available of suitable (safe) material for equestrian uses initially stalled. However, this left a big disposal problem, with attempts at incineration raising environmental issues, and landfill proving very expensive. Following the installation of expensive plant that can extract wire, fibred rubber safe for arena construction is once again available at an economical cost, although some granules may be smaller than was previously the case.

In respect of these last two points, we would reiterate the advice given in our Introduction to the second edition of this book:

> All-weather surfaces use both quarry-based materials and recycled materials in their construction. We would stress that careful selection and preparation of these materials is important, and that false economies should be avoided. The disposal of waste products, including those of tyre manufacturers and the plastics industry, is an expensive business. In consequence, there is a temptation for those with waste to dispose of to offer cheap materials, which are not of the quality required for arena construction. In recent times, material that was being rejected for use twenty years ago, for reasons of unsuitability or rapid failure, has been offered again. Make certain, therefore, that any material you select is fully suitable and has a long life.

Another factor that will impact on construction is that transport costs have increased all round. Therefore, sourcing *suitable* material locally, where possible, has even greater benefits, as does the appropriate use of construction techniques that require relatively low volumes of material.

From our own perspective, we would like to report, with some satisfaction, that our original arena, built in 1980 and featured on the front cover of the first edition, is still in use for showjumping and dressage. However, we, like others, are still learning about all-weather surfaces, and a major triumph has been the further development of the reinforced turf project, first outlined in the final chapter of the first edition, and explained in more depth in the second. While, as stated, it is the purpose of this book to explain *all* materials and methods relevant to the provision of artificial surfaces for horses, and while we do not intend it to be an advertisement for our own products, we do give more information on *Springway* ® projects in this edition. The reasons for this, in brief, are that we believe the *Springway Conduit Base System* to be a particularly effective system of addressing issues of drainage and water conservation, and the *Springway Fibre* turf reinforcement system is now established as a successful method of preserving turf from wear and permitting regeneration over large areas, and is in use at major venues such as polo grounds and eventing courses. We believe, therefore, that these projects are making a contribution both to the environment and to the safety and comfort of horses, which is surely the aim of all who install all-weather surfaces.

1.

Our Own Process of Discovery

IN THE EARLY 1980s, we needed an all-weather surface. At that time, the recommended method of construction was a membrane with a wood fibre topping. This was duly installed by us, but failed after eighteen months.

As a move to a new property was imminent and there was a need for an international size arena, we requested quotations from specialist contractors. These established the cost of installation, but the technical specifications seemed unsound. For example, the reasons given for use of membranes were suspect; also, the lifespan of suggested wood chip surfaces was being questioned by many of our equestrian friends who already had such surfaces installed.

During this time it became apparent that producers of industrial plastics were looking for a recycling outlet for their waste products. Therefore we decided to build a 60 x 25 m patchwork arena to test various grades of sand and plastic waste products in the hope of achieving a suitable surface.

The base construction was of equal importance and, as our move was to be from heavy New Forest clay to solid chalk, it was decided to test the latter as a base. Therefore, we dug the base down to the chalk, forming a slope for drainage across the 25 m width. We believed that any drainage through the base would be short-lived, and this proved to be true. Any run-off would be across the base and down the slope. The surface-retaining boards had a 50 mm clearance beneath to permit free run-off.

The base was then covered to a 50 mm depth with various grades of washed sand from local pits. These were laid as a patchwork for test purposes. As a reference, a 75 mm depth of wood chips was added to one area.

Several manufacturers supplied plastic waste materials and these were added as a further patchwork on top of the sand. Some of the materials were then found to be in limited supply when additional loads were ordered. However, one sample was of rubber-fibred pips; a waste product of mat manufacture. We were told that large quantities of similar material, but in larger pieces, were being disposed of by dumping down redundant mine shafts. Test work thus far had indicated that relatively large pieces of material provided a better surface than small pieces, so the matting manufacturer undertook to have waste fibre collected and granulated down to various sizes. Tested and mixed with various grades of sand, the first batch provided proved successful; it supported the horses well – they rode on top; it also added a resilience to the surface which had not been provided by other materials. Since we had entrance mats over thirty years old made of the same material we were satisfied that we were dealing with a long-life facility. Furthermore this surface was free-draining and completely all-weather.

As a result of this experiment, various personalities from the horse world asked to try the surface and then requested help with their own arenas.

Experience gained by helping others on their own sites established a basis for providing further information on all aspects of construction and choice of surface materials. In our continued research, we were assisted by experts from relevant fields.

The Chief Engineer of the rubber matting manufacturer established the best method of manufacturing the aforementioned fibre and his company agreed to produce it commercially for use on artificial surfaces. As a result, we agreed to help with the practical development of its use.

An experienced contractor, who had helped with the construction of our new stables and the base for a lunge arena, had been involved for some time in the installation of wood fibre arenas. At this point, however, he also was looking for an alternative method of construction. Therefore an arrangement was made to co-operate in experimental building.

It was agreed that the base was as important as the surface, and thus the need to design and test a complete specification became apparent. Furthermore, we had also learnt that it was essential to have a maintenance procedure that suited the particular method of construction. It was also concluded that, although the fibre used and method of construction remained the same, it was possible to tune the arena to meet particular needs by varying sand quality and maintenance procedures.

Our original all-weather arena at Village Farm, still in use twenty-four years after installation. A grit sand/fibred rubber surface on a sloping base for drainage. The inset shows the surface today.

In the interests of further research, we visited Essen Equitana, to learn what alternative surfaces were available. At that time interest in Germany was concentrated solely upon artificial surfaces for indoor schools: only 'mad dogs and Englishmen' rode outdoors in wet and freezing weather and required frostproof surfaces! Since we had developed such a system, we were encouraged to become involved in a marketing activity for the first time.

Our family's equestrian interest was mainly dressage and we had become keen supporters of Goodwood's efforts to create national interest in that discipline. Therefore, we selected Goodwood's International Championships as our first venue for a trade stand. This attracted considerable interest and, the following year, it was apparent that there had to be a more professional presentation. People had to be aware there was a long-life alternative to wood fibre available...

At about this time it became apparent that riding on the grass could no longer be permitted at Goodwood. The venue now needed three artificial surfaces if it was to run an International and a National Championship each year. (This illustrates the way growth in equestrian sport has made the use of artificial surfaces necessary.) That year, while we were at Essen Equitana, Lord March (Goodwood's owner) visited our stand and announced that we were being asked to rebuild the wood fibre arena at Goodwood before the next International. At the same time, a Spanish group asked for information on all-weather surfaces, having informed us that Barcelona had been selected as the venue for the Olympics in four years time.

Later that year, at the Goodwood International, there was a meeting of the Equestrian Committee, making final arrangements for the Seoul Olympics. They were interested in the relaid Park Arena and asked for information on various methods of arena construction.

Unfortunately, it seems that the arena builder at Seoul was not allowed to use imported material and, at Barcelona, although some rubber granules were added to make the surface more resilient, the drainage system failed to cope with local climatic conditions.

The Olympics is an example of the occasional need to install temporary outdoor arenas for major equestrian events, which may be in areas with little experience of outdoor arena construction. While different areas may require different solutions, arbitrary restrictions and failure to evaluate local conditions are unlikely to produce the best results. While it is to be hoped that major venues will have learnt lessons from the past, there is also a lesson here for the individual, who may have to live with the consequences of a decision for a number of years.

Reverting to our own experience, the interest in Goodwood's Park Arena led to a suggestion that we provide a temporary indoor arena for the British Equestrian Trade Association (BETA) Fair at Sandown Park. This created interest in the racing world and also support from an international firm of Civil Contractors. Their Racecourse Architect was nominated as our contact, to provide help with construction methods and communication with organizations such as the Jockey Club. This led to an involvement with the laying of all-weather gallops in Britain and an all-weather racetrack abroad.

Many enquiries to our trade stands at BETA and Goodwood were along the following lines:

We have installed a base and liner and now wish to buy the surface.

We then had to establish what type of base, and why a liner was being used. The enquirer had restricted their choice of surface and, in many cases, spent more money than a complete arena with matching base and surface would have cost.

We have installed a sand arena and the surface is blowing away.

We had to point out that, while a sand arena can be functional if it is kept watered, it is not an all-weather surface.

We have an arena which has no spring, can we add fibre on top?

After nearly twenty years of testing, learning, and answering this type of question, we believe it is time that a book is available which first, will help people select an affordable arena or gallop which will meet their needs and second, give them an understanding of the ongoing cost and maintenance work involved.

We believe that a good system has been developed, which can be used for all equestrian activities. Other systems which work well are also available. It is like buying a horse. You have to decide what you can afford, what is the best buy and whether you are willing to look after the surface you have spent your money on. Like a horse, an all-weather arena can give a lot of pleasure but, like a horse, it must be kept fit and usable.

2.

The Aim of an All-Weather Surface

I F WE TRY TO define the ideal riding surface, we consider a surface equivalent to the finest English turf, with a firm base, self-regenerating and usable under all weather conditions.

The properties of good turf are that it has free drainage, resilience, but does not give a deep ride. It has a surface which does not break away but gives good footing. It is self-regenerating with restricted use. Permanent turf with a deep root structure (to hold the surface together), on a firm level base (probably chalk or gravel sub-soil), can give a beautiful ride. The best example of good turf for equestrian use is downland turf on chalk. This has resulted in the racing industry being based in areas such as Newmarket and Lambourn. These locations tend to have a very limited depth of topsoil, 100–150 mm, on pure chalk. Chalk provides a level, concrete-hard base. There is some drainage through the base but also, in wet weather, good run-off as a result of elevation and slope.

The horse has evolved to perform on good turf and desert sand. On both these surfaces there is some cushioning effect to minimize jarring and, equally important, some forward movement of the foot on landing to give controlled deceleration. Both these properties help to keep the horse sound. If you examine the hoofprint of a horse on good going you will see that the hoof has depressed the turf and soil to about the depth of the shoe, and has also moved forward between 10 and 25 mm, depending on pace.

Mature turf has sufficient resilience to recover almost immediately. However, if overused, or used in very wet weather conditions, the protective top growth is destroyed, and the ground becomes poached. When the root structure has been destroyed, or overcompaction takes place, regeneration is no longer possible. Therefore, good turf has to be preserved by restricting its use to suitable weather conditions, controlling the amount of use and, most important of all, through periods of non-use, to permit natural regeneration.

What we are trying to achieve is a surface with all the good properties of turf, and none of the restrictions on use. In many situations this is far from easy but, if we agree to some element of periodic maintenance in place of natural regeneration, much of value can be achieved.

3.

General Principles of Construction

T HE FIRST SYNTHETIC surfaces that horses had to cope with were
roads installed to supply a surface for the wheel, or for marching
Roman Legions. In more recent historical times, it became popular to
school horses indoors, for dressage and airs above the ground. The first
artificial surfaces specifically for horses were therefore indoors. They
tended to be sand on a masonry base, although attempts were made to
provide more spring by adding heather or faggots to the sub-base. The
Spanish Riding School in Vienna is the most famous example but
others, such as at Wilton House, occur in England.

More recently, the porous fibre membrane was invented for road
construction purposes. This was intended to go under the base of roads
in clay areas, to spread the load and stop clay coming up into the base.
It was found that this membrane could also be used above a stone base
to separate a sand or wood chip topping from the base.

This system became the basis for arena and gallop construction at a
time when an increase in equestrian sport exceeded the availability of
good turf. In England, equestrian sport also became an all-year activity,
but without adequate indoor facilities being available. In the racing
world considerable advantage could be achieved by having a horse fit at
the start of the season. This led to the development of all-weather
gallops, again with sand or wood fibre surfaces. The first surfaces constructed soon ran into problems arising from poorly selected sites,

drainage systems failing, bases breaking up and a lack of appreciation that adequate maintenance procedures had to be established and followed. Few proved to be genuinely all-weather.

Alternative methods of construction and alternative surface materials were tried, both for gallops and arenas, and this process continues. Quite often a new surface will appear and it may take at least five years to establish effective life and all-weather properties. Often similar systems are offered under different brand names. This can make it difficult for someone trying to select an arena to meet their particular needs.

It is the purpose of this book to provide enough of the theory of artificial surface construction to help you understand information provided by vendors, and thus select a system which makes sense to you and meets your needs. There are four problems to resolve:

1. What sites are available and which one is most suitable?

2. What size of arena do you need, and what type of surface will meet your requirements?

3. What type of base is suitable for the site and surface selected?

4. Can you afford it?

We will discuss these matters in detail in the ensuing chapters but, for the moment, we can summarize the main principles as follows.

The Site

The arena is being installed to make it possible to ride in all weather conditions. This normally means that the arena should be as close to the stables as possible with easy, level access. However, the site selected should also permit economic construction of the arena or gallop. A large delivery of material in bulk carriers will be required and access from a good road is desirable. If the only site available has poor access, or access is across a field, timing of installation is crucial. Money will be saved if installation is in dry weather conditions, on dried-out ground. Therefore, if financial or access considerations necessitate, have the base installed in early summer, and the surface in the autumn. Any problems with the base will then have some time to show up and to be rectified before the surface is installed.

Size and Surface Material

Depending upon your personal requirements, size may either help dictate, or be dictated by, the site. It may also influence your choice of surface because, as we shall see, surfacing is costed not simply by area, but by volume.

Many types of surface are now available, but few are completely all-weather. Some are suitable only for particular types of equestrian activity. Some require considerable routine maintenance work, which may involve expensive equipment. Some will need watering. The life expectancy may be short before top-up and then renewal is necessary. The cost of surfacing can vary considerably per tonne, but volume is the important cost factor. Some surfaces will perform well laid 100 mm deep, others have to be 250 mm deep. Each type of surface will require a suitable type of base, and the cost of the base can vary considerably. You have to be clear about which equestrian activities you need the surface for, and the importance of surface availability in different weather conditions.

Take the opportunity to ride on as many surfaces as possible under different weather conditions before making your choice. If you find a surface in your locality (climatic conditions can vary considerably) which is over five years old, still working well, and provides the ride you want, this must be worthy of consideration.

The Base

Having selected the site and the surface, it is necessary to design and construct a base to link the two together. The base must be strong enough to stand up to impact damage, and spread the load to suit the site under all weather conditions. The surface must key to the base; the base must not break up and add unsuitable material to the surface.

With traditional systems of construction, provision must be made for disposal of surplus rainwater from the arena site (see also Chapter 7) and, whatever drainage system is adopted, the surface material must be prevented from blocking this system. It must also be remembered that all arenas are acting as filter beds. They will receive dust from the atmosphere, mud off horses' feet, and droppings.

The boom in arena construction was started with the discovery that membrane material designed to go under roads could be used as the interlayer to solve these problems. Unfortunately, it appeared to give a cheap means of construction, and many arenas were built with inadequate bases. Furthermore, there are two objections to the use of membranes in this way. First, as well as spreading the load, the membranes were designed to prevent fine clay-like materials from rising into road bases. If they do this, they will also filter out fine material which is travelling down, and clog. Second, with a membrane system, you have to protect the liner from the horses. This means a surface 250 mm deep, which can result in a surface which is too deep for the horses.

Cost

The size, location and method of construction will govern the capital cost of the arena or gallop. As a very rough guide, at least half the cost will go into a properly constructed base. With reasonable care this is a once-only cost, provided that the selected drainage system continues to work.

Most of the materials other than sand used for surfacing are recycled waste products. As first manufactured, they would have been far too expensive for arena construction. Many are in limited supply and have alternative uses, for example good quality wood chip is used for chipboard manufacture. For this reason alone it is worth having available alternative materials for arena and gallop construction. Furthermore, given the volume of material required to build an all-weather surface, transport is a significant cost factor. Using local materials when possible will reduce cost, but the material must be of the right quality.

The running costs will be: routine maintenance (which must be done), watering if necessary, the cost of top-up, and periodic surface replacement. You have to justify these costs and the capital cost against the improved opportunity to use and keep the horses fit, in a handy and safe location.

4.

Project Responsibility

WHEN UNDERTAKING any project, it is essential to define who is responsible. Building an arena is no different. If you decide to do it yourself, you are responsible and you have to decide whether the savings justify this. With proper equipment, two or three men can install an arena in seven days, provided the weather is suitable. Labour is a small part of the cost. To save money, you have to buy materials of the right grade as cheaply as a contractor can, and you must have available, or hire, suitable equipment. If you have to hire equipment on a day rate basis, you have to use it as efficiently as a contractor, who is motivated to achieve a profit margin.

Selection of the right grade of material, especially sand, is crucial. A contractor should select suitable material at the best price in your area, to minimize transport costs. If you have suitable material – hardcore for example – an option is to issue it free to the contractor when negotiating the price.

If you decide to use a contractor, it is preferable to choose one who provides the surface you have selected and a suitable base as a total package. He will do a site selection survey for you, provide a base to suit his surface, install the surface, and agree maintenance procedures with you. Periodic visits from him during the first few months commissioning will be an advantage, so that any minor problems can be corrected.

If you do not choose this course of action, there are various questions you must be prepared to answer. For example, who is responsible when offers to build to your specification are made, or an offer to provide just the surface, with a suggestion that you ask a local contractor to put in the base? Such alternatives should be considered with care.

Guarantees are nice to have, but cost money. They can cover different aspects, for example a guarantee may be for the life of material supplied, or the complete installation. The problem is that there can be a two- or three-way responsibility; selection of the surface to give the quality and availability of ride you require, quality of base design and installation, and, just as important, your ability to follow the maintenance procedures agreed. Most installations will last at least two years. The problem arises when the arena waterlogs, freezes in severe weather, or the surface dusts up and blows away in high winds. Who is responsible? For instance, in the last case, have you failed to water?

Your best guarantee is a contractor who has been installing arenas to a particular specification in your area for a long time, and cannot afford to have a failure. If you are wise, you will invite him to make a periodic visit to inspect and advise; you have a mutual interest in a successful arena.

Nothing sells an arena better than a five-year-old installation which a contractor is able to invite potential customers to ride on. If you arrange for such a contractor to provide a complete installation, it is well worth discussing a maintenance contract where he makes an annual visit, rectifies any problems before they become major, checks out your maintenance procedures, and recommends any top-up necessary.

5.

Site Selection and Survey

IN THE FOLLOWING pages, information will generally relate to arena construction. Later in the book there is a chapter specifically on gallop construction, where additional factors may apply. However, so far as site selection is concerned, special comment upon gallops is necessary. Horses visiting a gallop need a warm-up period before a full gallop. In this case, a safe approach track of suitable length from stable to gallop may be appropriate. Where possible, the stables should be in the valley, the gallop on the high ground above. At Newmarket, two 5 furlong warm-up tracks were initially installed to meet this need (there are now six all-weather gallops at Newmarket).

If your land permits you a choice of sites, it is worthwhile giving considerable thought to your selection. We would suggest that, in order of priority, you should consider the following points:

1. The most convenient location for use, as close to the stables as possible, with good approach and access under poor weather conditions.

2. Good drainage off the arena, with somewhere for the water to discharge to (see Chapter 7).

3. Will the land itself need draining? In this respect, you can be misled if you look at it in the summer only; you must consider winter conditions. We know of one arena which appeared fine when built in summer, but had a spring appear in the middle, in the winter.

4. Is there good access during construction, and for future maintenance?

5. Are there going to be cost savings by, for example, building on a chalk plateau, instead of down on a flat clay field? We originally had this choice and do not regret choosing the chalk.

The Severals warm-up track at Newmarket.

It is well worthwhile inviting any contractors you are considering using to participate in this review. They will dig a few holes to investigate site conditions for you, and give you alternative quotations. It also gives you a chance to check out their co-operation and competence.

We get many enquiries from people changing house and asking about an arena on a new site. This is a sensible approach. They are considering whether the new property is suitable for equestrian use. Is the old barn suitable for conversion to an indoor school? Can the concrete parking area be converted to an all-weather arena at low cost?

By following the points outlined, you should eventually end up with costed alternatives from which to select your best buy.

6.

Choice of Surface

ALTHOUGH THEY WILL be discussed in more detail in Chapter 7 we can, for the moment, consider surfaces in broad outline. There are basically three types of material available for arena surfaces. They are:

Sand and grit in many grades and sizes

All true sands are made of silica. So-called silica sand is just one type, generally light in colour and suitable for glass making. There are some materials which may look like sand, but can break down very easily, an example being mica.

Sand is often used on its own; it can also be used bonded together with monofilament synthetic fibres or oil additives.

Wood waste material; peelings, chips, fibre and shavings

These can originate from hard or soft wood. Some are offcuts from seasoned timber, furniture manufacture etc; others will be culled or wind-blown timber not suitable for manufacture, and could include rot-bearing material. An alternative use for the high quality material available is chipboard manufacture and, at times, it can be in short supply for arena construction. The other sources can be extremely variable in quality, with differing types of timber mixed together. Some timbers, such as larch, are rot-resistant and tough. Others will break down very quickly.

The range of grits
and sands that can
be used.

BELOW Close-up of a
wood fibre surface.

Wood chips and fibre are normally used on their own. Where they are used mixed with sand, breakdown can be very rapid owing to the abrasive nature of the sand.

Recycled waste product from plastic manufacture, or tyres

Much of the plastic which is used is sheathing recovered from electric cable. The plastic has been stripped off to recover the copper, but some samples may still have some fine copper wire present. The tyre material can be granulated rubber recovered from the tread, or canvas plus rubber recovered from the carcass. Most tyres now contain wire reinforcement. Tyres have to be carefully selected, broken down and granulated to produce suitable wire-free material. Expensive machinery installed in recent years does this quite efficiently, but the new processes mean that much of the material now available is smaller than was formerly the case.

Plastic- and rubber-based materials are normally used in combination with various grades of sand to modulate the qualities of the surface.

PVC granules recovered from cable.

Waste material
from mouldings.

Fibred rubber
recovered from
tyres.

Other waste products are tried from time to time, but few materials prove sufficiently durable or are available in sufficient quantity.

Drainage Properties of Surfaces

The speed at which water drains down through a surface is a function of material size and depth. Fine sands drain slowly and lock together when wet to give a firm surface. If there is clay present, or other very fine material such as broken down wood fibre, these can waterlog. With this type of surface, drainage has to be down through a porous base with a drainage system under (see Chapter 7). As you increase the material size, the drainage will improve. This can be done by increasing grain size and mixing in other material. Big wood chips used on their own will drain freely. With some materials it is possible to improve drainage to the extent where you can drain across the surface as well. When this becomes possible, you can drain across a sealed base, and no underdrain system is necessary, provided that the width of the arena is no greater than 30 m. (The *Springway Conduit Base System*, described in Chapter 7 and elsewhere, is capable of providing adequate drainage over a distance of at least 60 m.)

Sourcing Surface Materials

Experienced arena builders establish suitable sources of material in their area, and know the minimum cost of supplying adequate quality. This should be reflected in their quotation.

The two materials generally used in bulk are sand and wood fibre. In most locations to date, these have been obtainable within a short distance of the arena site. If this is possible, transport costs will be reduced, but the materials must be of suitable quality. It is always worthwhile asking for samples before ordering. These should be saved for comparison with the material which is finally delivered, just in case you should need recourse to the 'sale by sample' provisions of the Sale of Goods Act.

Sand has always been a particularly difficult material. It can be produced in various ways. It may be as dug from the pit, screened to size and remixed if necessary, or produced by crushing large rejects. It should be noted that a pit can be producing from different strata and the quality can suddenly change. Furthermore, sand usually has to be washed to eliminate clay and the efficiency with which this is done can vary considerably.

Recent experience has highlighted the current difficulty in sourcing sand suitable for arena construction. A long-standing local supplier of ours can no longer find, in this area, a pit willing to wash sand to the standard required for this use. The difficulty is that most pits are now under the control of international companies whose main business is the supply of aggregates for concrete manufacturing, and whose ultimate use for a worked-out pit is as a dry hole for waste disposal. These companies have little interest in the relatively small equestrian market, and no wish to wash their product beyond the demands of the British Standard for washed concrete and building sand. Since this Standard permits a large percentage by volume of fines contamination, the washing can be minimal. (There is no British Standard for equestrian sand.) An additional factor nowadays is that, under recent legislation, it is no longer permitted to wash silt into rivers; whatever the environmental advantages of this, it is a further disincentive for companies to produce clean sand cheaply. To this is added the fact that a tax on aggregates means that all sand is now more expensive than before.

Since, for arena construction, a supply of clean sand is needed, it is now more important than ever that the jar test (see Chapter 8) is used both to check samples submitted, and the material delivered against those samples.

The other point about sand is that, for an optimum surface, an appropriate blend of grain sizes is needed (the specific blend will depend upon the characteristics of the individual arena and site). The British Standard for washed concrete and building sand identifies three grades from 5 mm down: fine, medium and coarse. Within these grades it allows for a wide variation in percentage of grain size but, for equestrian use, the BS coarse and medium grades will usually suffice, provided that the overall quality is satisfactory.

It is impractical to list all the variations in type and size of materials that are used in arena construction. Sands and sand-based arenas come in all types; it is necessary to select the specification best suited to your needs. The plastic and tyre waste materials tend to be sourced from manufacturing facilities and granulating plants, and delivery may be over some distance. Since transport costs have risen considerably, this is a matter for consideration, which points to the use of construction methods that minimize the weight and volume of materials used. However, for smaller projects, transport costs may be less significant, since one lorryload of a material may be sufficient for your arena.

With some methods of surface construction it is better to premix the materials before laying. This reduces the time taken for the surface to lock together evenly and safely. On some sites, however, this may be difficult to do and it may be more economic to buy in premixed material. Sand, which is likely to be one component, has a high weight to volume ratio, so a typical 50:50 blend by volume specification may contain 80 per cent sand by weight. This fact should be reflected in the price.

The information above should suffice to indicate that there is no such thing as a standard wood fibre, sand, or sand blend arena surface and that, whenever possible, materials should be sourced locally to keep down the cost.

Once you have ridden on as many surfaces as possible and made your choice of surface, you then have to determine the type of base suitable for both your site and the surface you have selected. When the costs of surface and base are added together you will know the capital cost of your arena.

7.

The Base

L ET US ASSUME that the arena site has been selected and a survey has indicated any specific problems to resolve. The preferred surface has also been selected and now the base must be chosen and installed to act as the interlayer.

The base itself must be bigger than the proposed arena to avoid fall-away at the edges, and to hold pegs or posts required for the surround boards and rails.

Base below ground level

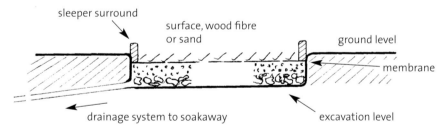

Base below ground level

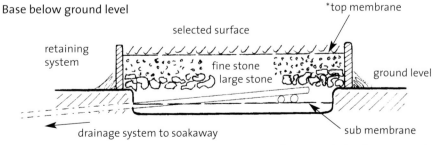

*common, but not recommended

Cross-sections through typical arenas.

For a while, it was standard practice to remove topsoil until a firm sub-base was found, the site being levelled by back-filling with hard-core. This could require a lot of material and generally resulted in a base below ground level, which could possibly create difficulties in providing an appropriate discharge from the drainage system. In many cases, the arena itself would become a drainage system, receiving water back from the adjacent land under wet weather conditions, just like a hole in the ground. Experience suggests that it is generally better and cheaper to build above the ground. On most sites this is possible, if necessary using a membrane system between ground and base.

In some cases, it will be necessary to cut and fill to achieve a level site. If so, it is essential to build up the low point in layers and consolidate to avoid future settlement.

On waterlogged sites, it may be necessary to install an under-base drainage system. The base should end up above the surrounding land on all four sides, with a relieving ditch or gulley on the high side. This should make it impossible for water to come onto the base from adjacent land. If there is a track leading into the arena this must also be protected by a ditch or ramp. (Our own development, the *Springway Conduit Base System* – described later this chapter – has a watertight

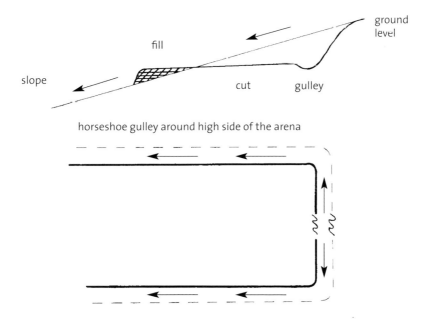

Ground preparation for the arena on a sloping site.

perimeter and can therefore be installed with a curb at ground level, provided that discharge from conduits to a drain or pond is possible.)

Most bases are built up with suitable local roadstone, starting with big material and capping with smaller material; you are building up a filter bed. However, when selecting the material for constructing the base, it is worth utilizing any available hardcore or brick rubble for the sub-base.

The base material must be frostproof because, in severe weather, a base can freeze and some quarried materials will break down on thawing. If chalk is used, care must be taken during a thaw because, once thawed, chalk locks back together as a concrete-like material. Any chalk used must be kept clean and free from contamination by soil or clay.

If you have selected a surface that requires drainage through the base, an appropriate drainage system must be incorporated in this base, above the liner (if used).

The aim is to produce a base surface which is level, solidly locked together, yet porous. It has to provide adequate drainage, but not let any fine material in the surface pass down into the base. If this happens, the drainage system will become sealed. This is difficult to avoid. Also, it is very easy for the base surface to break up and for stones to rise and contaminate the riding surface. Attempting to prevent this by locking the base together with fine material can impair the drainage.

It is for these reasons that a membrane may be used between base and surface. This has to act as a filter and can, itself, become sealed with fines or organic growth. If a membrane is used there must be adequate depth of riding surface to avoid damage to the liner by the horses. One experienced designer of arenas recommends a porous asphalt surface

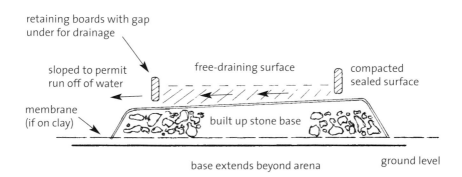

Cross-section through a sealed base arena.

to the base. If correctly installed, this provides adequate porosity, and sufficient mechanical strength to hold the base together. If you have selected a surface with properties that permit drainage across the base, the problem is simplified: you do not need a base drainage system, and the roadstone base can be sealed and locked together as in a road. As with a road, a slope (camber) is incorporated to encourage free drainage off the base. The surround boards have clearance underneath to permit free run-off to ditch or drain. This type of construction also has the advantage of sealing the ground under the arena from rainfall, a feature which should dry out and consolidate the base. If, however, you anticipate difficulties with water supply for watering the arena surface, you should consider the points made in the next section before deciding upon this option.

Experienced contractors have generally acquired sufficient skills to use local materials to provide a base which suits the type of surface they are offering. However, things can become difficult if you split responsibility between one contractor installing the base and another providing the surface.

Water Run-off and Conservation

The matter of water disposal and conservation requires a two-pronged approach during the construction of an all-weather arena.

During heavy rainfall, the amount of water affecting an arena-sized area will be considerable. For example, 1.25 cm (half an inch) of rain falling on a 60 x 20 m arena will mean that there are 15 cubic metres of water to dispose of – an amount that would fill a small swimming pool. This will have to be disposed of efficiently by the drainage system if it is not to compromise the usefulness (or structure) of the arena. Nor should it be forgotten that a covered school of the same size will have the same volume of water falling on the roof – so the guttering and drainage system must be able to disperse this properly.

The other side of the coin is evaporation from the arena surface during dry periods. During the summer, the rate of evaporation is likely to exceed water replacement through rainfall (this will obviously be true of indoor arenas). Since most all-weather systems need to be kept moist to bond the surface together, some form of water supply is required and this must be relatively clean if the surface is not to become adulterated. In some sites and circumstances a main supply can be quite expensive, so a system that conserves and reuses rainwater should be considered. It is possible to install a base system which incorporates a conservation reservoir in addition to the drainage system at relatively little extra cost, and we would recommend that this addition be given consideration.

Our Own Development

It was this premise that led us to carry out experimental work which looked at the water conservation issue from a slightly different angle. Our starting point was as follows. In most parts of the UK, given more or less 'normal' weather conditions, the total amount of water needed to retain an optimum surface (whether natural or artificial) approximates to the total amount of rainfall. In other words, if the overall rainfall could be 'metered out' as regular waterings, it would pretty much fulfil the watering need. In the past, however, arena design has been significantly concerned with the disposal of infrequent periods of heavy rainfall, with periodic watering being viewed as a separate issue.

Our personal remit was to see whether it was possible to design a base which met both needs: retaining moisture when required and providing adequate drainage to cope with periods of excessive rainfall. A trial arena was installed, and we evaluated its performance over a period to see whether the design objectives had been achieved.

We learnt a lot from this initial experiment. The base was installed at an inclement time of year, on a difficult site (a former builder's yard on puddle clay). A considerable amount of cutting and filling was necessary to level the site and concrete for the base was poured in very poor weather conditions. By completion, the water table was at base level and the drainage ditch had to be lowered to drain the site and take away the water from the conduit system. From this experiment, we learnt the need to have a suitable system to locate the conduits, the need for an elephant pump (see photo in following sequence) with adequate reach and the need for a rough tamped finish to key the surface to the base. However, despite the difficult conditions and the need for some rethinking, we confirmed that the method of construction of the base very cost-effective when compared to other base systems being used. There was a

The experimental base system.

The base.

Pre-mixing the surface.

BELOW Laying the surface.

reduction in the amount of plant required, and also of manpower. The work was carried out (as a planned part of the experiment) by a small local contractor with limited experience of arena construction, with help from the installer's family and friends. This indicated to us that the system was very easy to use, and that it could be very suitable for DIY installations. Most significantly, we had produced a successful arena on a difficult site. Concrete was proved to be a suitable base material and the surface, with a high ratio of fibred rubber to sand, soon stabilized to provide a resilient surface that could be maintained by a light roller. Now, three years on, it continues to give good service.

Following on from this first experiment, we used similar methods to install a second, 60 x 20 m arena, suitable for Grand Prix dressage. This time, we approached a very competent local civil engineering firm to manage the project, with the stableyard's owner and staff providing assistance. On this occasion, we learnt a lesson applicable to all arena installations. The first quotation we received was high, and included the costs of importing a large quantity of roadstone. However, we soon realized that, by rotating the arena through 90 degrees from its original orientation, a better layout was possible, which eliminated the need to import material and saved a lot of money. (It also enhanced the suitability of the arena for competition purposes, since the revised orientation offered better viewing for spectators!)

This second arena makes use of a clean pond to provide water conservation and pump-back facilities. This has produced savings on watering and maintenance costs. So far, it has proved possible to shut off the drainage system for most of the summer months; it is also possible, when necessary, to flood up the surface for levelling and regeneration.

Another feature of this arena is that we have provided a *Springway Fibre* reinforced turf (see Chapter 19) ride-in track around the perimeter.

While this second arena has been a great success, we once again learnt lessons during its construction. We discovered that four-way connectors would be a better way to join the conduits and provide a watertight system, and these, and the conduits, are now made of recycled plastic. We have also had manufactured special metal hair pins to locate the conduits. These features are now part of what has become the patented *Springway Conduit Base System*, which is now being marketed commercially.

Construction of the international dressage arena.

Site preparation – the plastic liner being laid.

Conduits installed and concrete base laid.

The elephant pump.

The curb being laid – note wash out plug on conduit system.

The premixed surface being laid.

The clean pond that was incorporated into the system.

The first test ride – note *Springway Fibre* laid on the ride-in track before reseeding.

The finished arena.

8.

Material Migration

As we saw in the previous chapter, with most arena systems you are building up a filter bed, starting off with big material and using this to support smaller and smaller materials in layers. Eventually, you end up with the surface on which you wish to ride. However, as in your garden, the bigger materials – the 'stones' – tend to rise to the surface. The horse in action is a very good vibrating machine and can speed up this process. Thus there will be some element of regeneration and remixing if equine feet penetrate down into the surface. This is why any large material which breaks away from the base will rise to the surface, and why any materials used in the arena will tend to segregate and layer out.

There is a simple test you can do that will demonstrate this. We call it the jar test. If you are purchasing sand, a glass jar with a watertight lid can be very useful for checking grain size and cleanliness. Fill the jar two-thirds full with the sand, cover with 25–50 mm of water, shake the jar and leave to settle. The sand will settle out in layers. Any clay or very fine material will settle on the bottom. If there is a mixture of grain sizes these will layer out, with the bigger material on top. The water may stay coloured for a considerable time, with ultra-fine organic material in suspension. This will ultimately settle as a waterproof sludge on the surface.

You can check out the surface of an arena and judge how contaminated the surface is becoming with fines from breakdown of materials, dust from the atmosphere, droppings, etc. in the same way. Take a representative sample through the surface and carry out the test. If the arena surface has a blend of materials; monofilament fibres, wood fibre or shavings, plastic or rubber granules, rubber and canvas, the same thing will happen as is demonstrated in the jar. Any very fine or

Testing sand

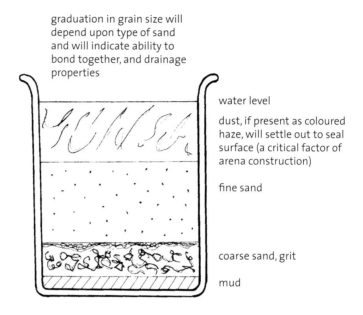

graduation in grain size will depend upon type of sand and will indicate ability to bond together, and drainage properties

water level

dust, if present as coloured haze, will settle out to seal surface (a critical factor of arena construction)

fine sand

coarse sand, grit

mud

Testing a typical arena surface

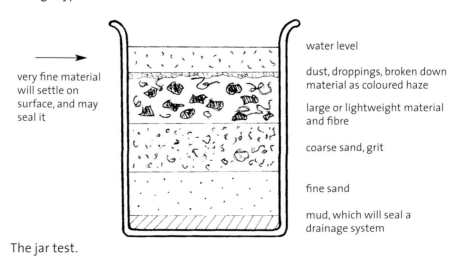

very fine material will settle on surface, and may seal it

water level

dust, droppings, broken down material as coloured haze

large or lightweight material and fibre

coarse sand, grit

fine sand

mud, which will seal a drainage system

The jar test.

lightweight material which comes to the surface will tend to blow away as dust. Monofilament will rise to the surface and, if allowed to dry out, will blow away, as will wood shavings. However, if the material which comes to the surface is of a sufficient size and weight, it can stabilize the surface (simulating grass) and provide resilience.

Any clay-like material which settles on the base of the jar during testing will do the same in the arena, with the potential to damage the drainage system. (While we have recently found a source of grit sand which is clay-free, this can contain a small percentage of mica, which breaks down into a white powder and has to be washed out, or else it will cause a dust problem if the surface is not kept moist.) Assuming that the arena has been properly constructed, the mode of failure of all surfaces is the same. The materials used in the construction break down to produce fines. Additional fines are being added by dust, mud off maintenance equipment, horse dropping, etc. Eventually, the material is unable to support the weight of the horse and/or the drainage system fails. Therefore, the maintenance system must incorporate rotovation if it is necessary to keep the materials mixed.

The life of an arena can vary considerably, depending upon durability of materials used, amount of use, and correct main-tenance procedures.

9.

Maintenance Procedures

ALL ARTIFICIAL SURFACES need maintenance. On this will depend the quality of ride, the effective life of the arena and the frequency with which it can be used. It can be a more significant cost factor than the initial capital cost. In selecting your arena, you have to look at the cost over say a ten-year period. If you are looking for a guarantee, this will take account of your obligations; if the surface needs watering, you must water it.

Maintenance procedures must take account of weather, type of use, and amount of use. Weather conditions will affect, for example, frequency of watering. Type and amount of use will govern the frequency of levelling, harrowing, or rolling – whichever is appropriate.

An important factor is the relationship between surface area and type of use. A riding school arena will get intensive use, possibly follow-the-leader type tracking. A dressage arena will get intensive tracking. A racetrack has an enormous area and very limited use per square metre, but it may still need intensive maintenance between each race because of the specialist surface selected. In all cases, it is always worthwhile using as much of the surface as possible by changing track. For dressage, an arena 25 m wide is advantageous – you can change the track and not continually have to ride the boards. If a flat surface is used for lungeing, a high level of maintenance may be required. This can be minimized by continually changing the centre point by walking slowly as you lunge.

(UPPER) Premixed fibre rubber surface (laid on a *Springway Conduit Base*), rolled to provide a good surface with (LOWER) minimal kick-back.

At the selection stage, it is a good idea to establish a maintenance schedule for a particular need; a riding school may have to schedule lessons to permit two half-hour maintenance periods per day.

While all need keeping level, different types of surface require different treatments. Some, such as the monofilament-bonded sand, will need periodic rotovation to keep the fibre mixed. This may also apply to blended materials, for example PVC with fibre. Other materials, such as fibred rubber, have relatively large particles which tend to stay on top by natural regeneration. Furthermore, a high ratio of fibred rubber in the mix can be used to lay a surface of relatively low volume. In addition to providing a very resilient surface, this permits the use of a roller to keep it level, rather than harrowing to break up the surface. By contrast, surfaces bonded together by water, wax or oil-based materials, will compact to give a 'dead' ride. These need harrowing or rotovating to keep the surface open for drainage, and to fluff it up.

Surfaces designed to drain across the base, with large, resilient material on top, normally require to be levelled in a way which causes as little interference with natural regeneration as possible. This type of surface consolidates to be suitable for flatwork first, and for jumping after some use. For speed work on gallops and racecourses, it can be lightly rolled to modulate the going.

Any arena perimeter will tend to build up surplus material. This must be returned to the adjacent track whenever necessary. Most surfaces require a minimum depth either to protect the liner, or to prevent surface material being crushed between horse and base.

The other main maintenance factor is how often you will need to top up or replace the surface. Again, this will vary according to material, usage and the efficiency of interim maintenance. Advice given under the terms of a good maintenance contract may be your best guide.

10.

Maintenance Equipment

MAINTENANCE EQUIPMENT can range from the simplest to the most elaborate. One of the best private arenas has been maintained with a light aluminium shovel – a few minutes work each time the arena has been used. There is generally a choice between equipment mounted on the hydraulic system of a tractor, or that towed on a loose link behind tractor or horse. The rigid type of levelling equipment, that is towed from a solid bar, is fine in professional hands for first construction or rectification work. However, real skill is necessary for correct use, otherwise it is very easy to turn minor ripples into humps and bumps.

If the arena is level, loose-link, free-drag equipment (towed by chain or wire), will level out hoofprints without affecting the grading of the surface.

If the surface is of a type which only requires levelling, very simple equipment is all that is necessary – a piece of wire-reinforcing mesh nailed to a jump pole, towed by a rope attached to each end of the pole, or perhaps a farm gate on a similar rope. There are purpose-made versions on the market, some of which incorporate a blade. Such implements can be used to clear material from the perimeter boards.

If the surface needs harrowing to keep it loose, you need a similar free-towed harrow with fixed or spring tines. Make sure that the tines are short and can only penetrate to the depth required. It is very easy to rip up the base, so beware the farmer friend with 250 mm spikes!

If the surface requires remixing, you need specialist rotovating

The tractor-mounted maintenance roller used for the Severals warm-up track.

The simple, low-cost maintenance system used on a typical above the ground arena at Easterton Farm, Perth.

equipment, which is very expensive and may be short-lived, because you are rotovating abrasive sand.

If the surface needs rolling, a lightweight, plain or ridged roller can be used on its own or incorporated in the drag system.

Don't forget the perimeter boards; it is often easier to clear these about once a month with a shovel. If the surface is a blend of materials, make sure you throw both materials back on the track, and that free run-off under the boards has been maintained.

When heavy watering is required regularly, a sprinkler system will be necessary. If damping down only is required for dust control, a bowser system may be cheaper. There are also systems available for under-surface watering. These could prove worthwhile, but you need to find out how much water is lost directly into the drainage system, as water is expensive and not always available. Beware of the local pond; you have spent a lot of money on clean materials and, without care, your unfiltered water source could contaminate the surface.

It is essential to avoid bringing mud and dirt onto the surface with equipment and horses. A proper approach track into the arena is required to avoid this.

11.

Why and When an Arena Fails

ALL ARENAS WILL FAIL in time. As we saw in the Chapter 8, this is generally caused by breakdown of surface material and the addition of other contaminating material. The first symptoms are failure to drain, riding deep, or dust problems. A small amount of dust coming off a surface is not normally a problem – in fact it is helping to prolong the life of the arena by clearing fines. However, severe dustiness must always give cause for concern.

Another cause of actual or effective failure is if the purpose for which the arena is being used changes. In this case the surface may no longer be suitable and unsuitable use will hasten failure.

In some cases, addition of plastic- or rubber-based material to a sand arena may help. Generally, however, it is better and more economical to replace the surface. Adding good material to failed material is a waste of money; and the arbitrary mixing of materials (for example, adding anything but wood fibre to wood fibre) solves nothing.

At the point of failure, it is worthwhile considering alternative surfaces. Having selected your new surface, and a suitable contractor, have the old surface removed, check the liner (if fitted), also the base and drainage system. This may identify the reason for failure. Rectify the problems, or have the base modified to suit the new surface. The cost of surface replacement is usually about 50 per cent of the cost of a new arena.

In some cases, it may be economical to clean up the existing surface by back washing or lifting the surface and screening to wash out the fines. With an across-the-base drainage system, the contaminated material may have caused the drainage system to fail by plating the base: this can form a ridge which stops drainage down the slope. In such a case it is a simple matter to push back the surfaces, blade off the ridge and replace the surface.

One example of 'retrieving' a failing surface occurred when a recently installed grit sand/fibre rubber surface failed to drain properly and, in very wet weather conditions, was not fit to ride on. A jar test (as recommended in Chapter 8) identified the fact that some of the sand supplied had not been pre-washed to appropriate standards.

A rectification programme of washing the sand clean in situ removed a considerable amount of fine material, which washed off the sand as a brown slurry. This cleaning was assisted by a period of very heavy rainfall.

Since being cleaned up in this way, the surface has performed to an acceptable standard, proving that early diagnosis and remedial action can avert a potential disaster. Incidentally, a post-cleansing jar test showed that the depth of silt had reduced from 5 mm pre-cleansing to 2 mm; evidence that this simple test has a crucial role to play in monitoring the condition of a surface.

12.

Construction Alternatives – an Overview

So far, we have dealt with the basics of construction and maintenance in broad principle. In this chapter, we shall compare alternative materials, construction and maintenance methods and costs in more detail.

From the points so far discussed, it will be apparent that every installation needs individual evaluation. Factors which must be considered are:

1. site conditions

2. local climate

3. type of use – whatever discipline(s) the surface is used for, it must support and protect the horses concerned.

4. all-weather properties

5. life

6. operating costs

Perhaps most important of all, what can you afford to spend? Is the installation value for money?

Any arena needs a properly constructed base and this tends to fix a minimum first cost of about £15 per square metre at 2004/5 prices. With some systems, the cost can rise to £30 per square metre. In between, there are many variations; the selected site can be a major factor. To provide some guidance the three main types of material used are examined below in approximate order of cost (see also the Table below). The order of cost assumes that the type of base normally used for that type of surface would be incorporated. There is also general comment on the properties of the type of surface each will provide, but note that there are infinite variations; size of material being the main factor. In our own work with the rubber fibre system we found that, although the same raw material was always used, particle size could, and sometimes must, be changed. For example, we found it necessary to change the specification used in Scotland from that in the South of England. What happens is that the local agent builds up knowledge of how to use local materials to build the base. The sand used may have to be blended to produce optimum drainage to suit local weather conditions. The same situation applies to all types of surface.

Comparative Costs of Sand, PVC and Rubber Materials

Material	£ per tonne	Approx. tonnes per cubic metre	£ per cubic metre
Sand	12.50	1.60	20.00
Wood fibre	35.00	0.30	19.20
PVC	25.00	0.80	20.00
Rubber	250.00	0.80	200.00
Fibred rubber	70.00	0.50	35.00
50:50 PVC/Sand *	23.70	1.10	24.53
50:50 Fibred rubber/Sand*	35.20	0.85	30.00

* by volume

NOTE: This table is a guide, based upon 2004/5 prices and average weight of materials. The weight of a volume of sand can vary by up to 25%, depending upon water content. It is essential that the sand is of the correct grade; it should be washed if necessary to ensure that there is no contamination with clay or dust-forming materials. The cost of sand now includes an aggregate tax.

Processed PVC and rubber-based materials will have varying weights per volume depending upon particle size.

None of the costs given includes transportation or VAT. At the time of writing, transportation generally adds about £10 per tonne to costs given.

A typical all-weather dressage arena.

The all-weather showjumping arena at Carluke, used for many Scottish competitions.

The crucial factor is how these materials work together to provide the surface you require. The required depth can vary from 100–250 mm, depending on the base used and the surface required, thus the volume required is a significant factor in the total cost.

Sand

Sand comes in many types and sizes. Most of the preferred sands are from land-based deposits, laid down by glaciers or rivers. This process has resulted in stratification into layers of differing sizes. A lot of sand is now sea-dredged. In some cases, such sand will contain significant quantities of shell. Shell is composed mainly of chalk and this can break down very quickly to chalk dust.

Suitable sand is becoming quite expensive, but the dominating factor can be cost of transport. If you are a long way from a suitable source it can be an expensive material. Sand arenas are normally laid deep, so the volume of material required is large. Sand arenas simulate a seashore and show the same properties. When damp, you have a firmly locked together structure and the horse can work 'on top'. When dry, you have a sand dune; the surface will ride deep and can blow away. For this reason, sand arenas are normally watered to maintain quality of ride and to preserve them. They tend to have a dead surface, but this can be mitigated by frequent harrowing. This must be done with short tines set to the correct depth, but the tines can be incorporated in the system used for levelling.

Sand itself will have a long life, but fines will build up and may eventually seal the drainage system.

Sand is normally a major constituent of blended surfacing systems, and any failures we have had have been the result of poor sand selection or inadequately washed sand. The grade of sand, grain size and mixture of grain sizes affect drainage characteristics and the amount of bonding that occurs. The type of sand selected must take into account location, rainfall, type of base, and the other materials used in the surface. There is no such thing as a sand that is suitable for all installations. Furthermore, given the variables involved, it makes sense to check each lorry-load prior to use.

Wood

Wood, again, comes in many types and sizes. Wood suitable for structural use costs in excess of £200 per cubic metre. For arena construction we are using a waste product material from various sources. It can be processed into various forms; peelings, fibre, chips or shavings. Generally it is used on its own, laid deep, but compacting down with use and breakdown. Again, you are dealing with a large volume of material and transport costs are important.

Some types of wood are rot-resistant and tough; others will break down quickly. Some culled timber may already have rot-producing organisms present. The best source will be offcuts from construction timber, but this has other uses and may not always be readily available.

Wood can provide a good riding surface. It first gets better with use, but then deteriorates as breakdown occurs. The surface can break away, so it is not normally used where fast turns are required; showjumping against the clock, for example.

On average, a wood surface needs topping up every two years. You reach a point where breakdown of material produces a lot of dust, and watering becomes necessary. The fines build up under a deep surface and, after five years, it is better to strip the surface, check the base and re-lay a new surface. If this is not done, a horse can suddenly break through the upper surface of good material into weak material beneath. Damage to the horse may result.

Maintenance will entail keeping the surface level with a drag, and watering in very dry weather.

Plastic- and Rubber-based Surfaces

These are other waste product materials which, when first made, may have cost £1,000 per tonne. Depending upon recovery and reprocessing costs they will still be expensive materials; up to £250 per tonne.

If you have a good sand arena of the right type, it is possible to add this type of material to improve the going. It will not significantly change the maintenance and watering requirements of the original arena.

These materials, generally blended with sand, can also be used to build new arenas. In this case a high ratio of plastic or rubber to sand may be used to create a relatively thin surface laid on a specialist base such as porous asphalt or a *Springway Conduit Base*; a combination which can provide a more resilient weatherproof surface.

Maintenance will consist of dragging to maintain a level surface. Generally the material is small, as recovered (for example, PVC stripped from domestic power cable). This means that the surface needs locking together with water or, in some cases, an alternative substance. Until recently, oil-based additives were commonly used, but wax has been found more satisfactory. It should it be noted no oil-based additives – including petroleum waxes – should ever be mixed with rubber materials such as tyre waste, since they will dissolve the rubber and produce an emulsion. There should, however, be no need to attempt to lock rubber in this way. The recycled tyre material is broken down into relatively large pieces, with the fibre exposed to simulate the root structure of turf. On the appropriate base, and blended with grit sand, you have a free-draining surface, which does not bond together on freezing. The

A fibred rubber and grit sand arena.

Fibred rubber and grit sand in close up.

large material size means that the horse rides on top; the high rubber content provides spring for a resilient ride. It is an expensive material to manufacture, but this is compensated for by the smaller amount used and its long life, so a complete installation is financially competitive.

Normal maintenance of the rubber/grit sand surface is achieved by dragging, which keeps it level. With this surface, it is particularly important to clear material back from the boards to a set level, which will maintain drainage under the boards. The minimum depth of surface must be maintained on the track. Watering is not normally necessary for flatwork, but the surface can be made firmer and faster by damping and rolling. In this condition, it is suitable for top level showjumping and racing.

Sand Bonded with Monofilament Fibre

This is a relatively expensive surface as the fibre is not a waste product. It provides a very firm surface which requires watering, and rotovating with specialist machinery, to provide the depth of riding surface required. It will recompact quickly and needs frequent machining.

Oil-bound and Wax-bound Surfaces

As mentioned in the section on plastic- and rubber-based surfaces, it is possible to use oil-based materials as an alternative to water to bond surfaces together, and oil can also be used for dust control. These surfaces tend to be very expensive because a considerable volume of bond material is needed. Very highly refined products should be used because of the environmental and health hazards involved. Test work we have done on such materials suggests that, while the oil locks dust and droppings together very effectively, they may clog the surface, and periodic re-oiling will be necessary.

Further to this issue, there was a proposal several years ago to use an oil additive for dust control on The Severals warm-up track at Newmarket. As this would have affected the guarantees, we decided to test the treatment on a lunge arena with an identical surface. The oil selected was environmentally safe, and it was added gradually until adequate dust control was achieved.

The surface worked well for twelve months but, in wet weather conditions, the oil started to combine with dust and water to form a slurry. The horses became very dirty.

It became necessary to clean up the surface and, with the very small area involved, this was possible. Using a hose with a jet nozzle, it was possible to wash the slurry (which was rather like emulsion paint), down to the central drain. Thirty hours work produced a clean-as-new surface with little sign of oil. Advice was given to water with a bowser if dust was a problem.

We believe this experiment reinforces the view that all surfaces fail as a result of fines building up and that attempts at dust control by bonding with the use of glue-like materials will speed up this process. Further additives will be needed once the oil's capacity to bond fines

Sand and waste material
bonded with wax.

BELOW Horse Guards Parade:
Eurotrack wax-bound surface
on asphalt base.

together is exhausted. The dust particles are locked into an oil/water emulsion, which seals the drainage system and can lead to premature failure of the surface.

With oil-bound surfaces, depending upon the degree of bonding, it may be necessary to rotovate to produce a good riding surface.

Recently, wax has replaced oil as a bonding agent and there have been many satisfactory installations. Indoors, it can provide a very good surface, but it does not eliminate the need to water for dust control. There is also a need for the periodic addition of more wax.

13.

Summary of Arena Selection Procedure

I N THIS CHAPTER we will emphasize the main points to consider when undergoing the process of selecting an arena.

1. List the purposes for which you wish to use the arena, and establish the minimum suitable size: 40 x 20 m is normal for novice dressage; 60 x 20 m for advanced dressage. For showjumping, a minimum width of 25 m is necessary.

2. Ask yourself whether you can afford to make it larger to avoid riding the boards continually, by making changes of 'outside track'.

3. How important to you is all-weather potential? Consider wet, dry, and frosty conditions.

4. What types of surface are being used for the purposes you have in mind? Check out major competitions, riding schools in your area and arenas in private use.

   The amount the arena is used may have a crucial effect upon lifespan. A wood fibre arena may be fine for private use, although its lifespan will be limited by rot potential. However, heavy use in a riding school could give a much shorter life, owing to breakdown of the wood fibre.

5. Having listed suitable surfaces, take every opportunity to ride on them to form your own opinion. Look at the maintenance procedures being used, the need to water, etc.

6. Talk to a variety of vendors. At this stage, you have to decide whether you want a contractor to take total responsibility for the project, or whether you intend to go it alone. If you are going to co-ordinate the project yourself, define the total specification and cost before starting.

   If you are going to place responsibility with a contractor, try to maintain a competitive tendering situation with alternatives. Establish the total capital cost of the project. Initially, budget prices are sufficient to screen out alternatives; when you have narrowed your choice, selected contractors can be requested to visit the site and give full quotations.

   Note that site selection may be very significant. Moving an arena a metre or two, or changing the shape or size, may avoid a lot of problems and save a lot of money. Using the knowledge gained from this book, you should be able to judge the competence of a contractor.

7. At this stage, it is essential to agree with the contractor the methods of maintenance necessary, the need to water and the capital cost of equipment required.

8. Having established total capital outlay, agree the method of payment, and establish any guarantees. (It would be normal to expect some method of phased payment.) It is worth remembering that any guarantees given will be conditional on you carrying out agreed maintenance. Also, will the contractor still be in business in five or ten years time?

9. Look at any ongoing operating costs; frequency and cost of watering, levelling, harrowing, or rotovation. Consider whether you can carry these out yourself. The frequency and type of these activities will vary with arena use and type of surface. The need to top up or replace the surface over a ten-year life cycle, and the cost of doing so, should be established.

From this evaluation you establish total cost over a period and your ability to afford it. For anyone who has already invested a significant amount of money in horses the answer to the question of affordability will generally be 'yes', unless suitable all-weather riding facilities can be hired nearby at reasonable cost. Remember, you must be able to keep a fitness and work programme for a horse proceeding without interruption and one fall on an icy road may prove costly in many respects.

If, at the end of the evaluation, owing to cost or site, you have no satisfactory solution, consider alternatives. A lunge arena can be built for about half the cost of a 40 x 20 m arena, on a space 13 m minimum in diameter. A lunge arena has many uses, which are explored in the next chapter. Alternatively, if you have a suitable area of grass, reinforcing it with fibred rubber could provide a suitable area for working when ground conditions would otherwise be too hard. (A means of reinforcing turf in this way is described in Chapter 19.)

Assuming that you are in a position to proceed with installation of an arena, the following general points will help ensure efficient and cost-effective installation and maintenance.

1. You will get a better arena for a lower cost if you plan ahead and have the installation completed under good weather conditions. It may be possible to agree with the contractor a phased installation; the base installed in early summer, the surface before winter.

2. The quality and type of base are crucial. If you get the base right, you have a very long-term investment. If a particular type of base is recommended for a surface, use it.

3. Generally, it is economical to include in the specification all extras required; watermain excavation, fencing, gates, etc.

4. The need to keep the arena clean by providing good, clean access for horses and maintenance equipment has been stressed. Appropriate access can often be installed at the beginning of the project, which will also provide good access to the site for construction equipment and materials.

5. Most surfaces require careful riding-in and some element of consolidation. The first heavy rainfall can work wonders. Get your maintenance procedures working as soon as possible, and step up the frequency initially; rolling may help. Restrict use to flatwork, with no sharp turns until the surface has consolidated. Care at this stage will pay dividends later.

6. If there are signs of problems, advise your contractor and invite him to pay a visit when next in your area; an early solution will save money. If your maintenance system needs modifying, the sooner you know, the better. A good arena is one installed by a happy contractor for a happy owner.

14.

The Value and Construction of Lunge Arenas

A LUNGE ARENA IS A MOST useful facility in its own right. It can be used for backing, exercise, as an emergency operating theatre and for controlled turning out. For safety reasons it needs a solid palisade and this means that a horse can be isolated from other distractions while being trained. Once you start getting a horse fit, it is essential to keep up the exercise despite inclement weather, otherwise health problems can arise. Controlled rehabilitation is also possible in a lunge arena. Therefore, while useful as an addition, a lunge arena should also be considered as an alternative if space is not available for a larger arena, or if funds are limited. Generally, the lunge arena can be located close to the stables on level ground. This means that it is always available in the worst of weather.

A lunge arena is the toughest test of surface material. The surface is being used for track work in a small area and there will also be an increase in dung loading if it is used as a turn-out area. Any surface can be considered but, because the horse may be moving at speed on a tight circle, good footing is essential. The problem of loose footing can be minimized by a coned base. The slope can be quite steep, bowl-shaped and to a central drain. With the correct slope, the risk of surface break-away resulting from centrifugal force can be reduced, and maintenance simplified.

Although construction above the ground is preferred, base and palisade are subject to strong bursting forces, and the design must reflect this.

Maintenance is normally carried out by dragging or hand raking to maintain an equal depth of surface down the slope. Watering may be necessary for dust control.

The minimum practical diameter for a lunge arena is 13 m, although 15 m is better. These dimensions are such that semi-indoor location within an existing barn may be possible.

15.

Construction of Gallops and Racecourses

I N THIS CHAPTER, we will look at general points relating to the construction of gallops, many of which are pertinent to the construction of actual racecourses. However, major issues relating to the present and future construction of racecourses will be dealt with in Chapter 16.

Since a gallop is narrower than an arena, lessons learnt in the construction of the latter can be of value when building the former. However, to reverse the process is difficult; lessons learnt from building a gallop have limited value when constructing an arena.

We have already indicated that the factors to consider when selecting a gallop site can be different from those for an arena. First, a location at a sufficient distance from the stable to permit the horses to warm up before doing speed work is desirable. If this is not possible, a warm-up facility similar to that provided at Newmarket is an alternative. Second, rising ground is desirable, so that the horses can be trained on varying gradients. Indeed, most gallops run uphill.

The artificial surfaces available are similar to those already described. However, a gallop tends to be used less per area of surface than an arena, but normally at a full gallop. The normal width is 3–4 m, but the wider the better, in that this allows horses to simulate a race situation, coming upsides and overtaking. Since width and speed of use will not permit sharp turns, breakaway of surface is unlikely, and wood fibre becomes an acceptable option.

The method of base construction will be similar to that of an arena.

Acceptable 'kick-back'. below knee height and not dusty.

A fibred rubber gallop being test-ridden for the Jockey Club.

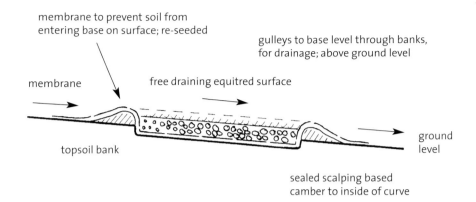

membrane to prevent soil from
entering base on surface; re-seeded

gulleys to base level through banks,
for drainage; above ground level

membrane

free draining equitred surface

topsoil bank

ground
level

sealed scalping based
camber to inside of curve

Cross-section through The Severals track.

The narrow width makes any drainage problem easier, but you can exchange the 'hole in the ground' problem of the arena for another. Because of the narrow width, long length and slope, it is very easy to create a 'river bed'. In heavy rain, water will tend to run down the track. This can lead to saturation at the low point, and the migration of surface material down the slope. Therefore, it is essential to allow run-off at frequent intervals down the track. This can be facilitated by the gallop being on a diagonal across the rising ground, or by introducing curves and bends. Constructing the base above the ground also avoids this problem.

At full gallop, and with more than one horse on the track, 'kick-back' can be a problem. Different surfaces kick up in differing ways. Sand surfaces bonded together by water, oil, or monofilament fibre tend to kick up in lumps. This can be minimized by frequently machining a loose surface onto the bonded surface. At a full gallop, this layer is recompacted on use, and it will therefore need remachining at frequent intervals. Surfaces built with large-particle material (woodchips and rubberized fibre) kick up in individual pieces. However, because these materials are relatively light and have good wind resistance, the energy stored is low, and is quickly dissipated. This means that such materials tend not to fly above knee height and have limited effect upon impact.

Most gallops are watered to produce a fast surface, and the use of a bowser is an option. If required, combined drainage and watering systems can be incorporated into the base. This is of special value in dry areas, where the conservation of water is an important factor. The back-wash facility can also assist by removing wind-blown fines. Most gallops are maintained by specialist equipment to suit the surface, being roto-vated, harrowed or rolled. If the surface is prone to freezing, rotovating may be carried out to keep the surface usable during the freeze period. Wax-bonded surfaces have proved successful on gallops, and minimize the need to water.

A racecourse has to have a surface similar to a gallop but, being the approximate width of a dressage arena, it needs the same drainage facilities. A racecourse will have cambered bends, so a drainage system suitable for the straights will work on the bends.

With some all-weather surfaces now being used on racecourses, there is an advantage in using such surfaces for training. If so, they need to be maintained to the same standard and by the same methods as the racecourse itself. It should be noted that racecourse surfaces are nor-mally remachined after each race, a process which demands investment in sufficient equipment to cover the whole track in less than the half-hour period between races.

16.

Racecourse Surfaces – the Past and Future

Although horseracing is the most publicly exposed equestrian sport, it is the one in which least progress has been made in the development of all-weather surfaces. To some extent, given factors related to speed and the forces generated by galloping horses, this is understandable. Nevertheless, one has to think that there is scope for greater development in this area.

The Position to Date

Traditionally, racing in Britain has taken place on natural turf, hence the establishment of Newmarket Heath as the focal point of flat racing, and areas such as Epsom, Lambourn and the South Downs as training centres. However, despite its excellent properties, the drawback with turf as a racing surface is that it requires periods of regeneration between use. To some extent, this has been dealt with in Britain by the limited use of a large number of courses, but this is not very cost-effective, and cannot counteract climatic conditions which leave large areas of the country either frozen or waterlogged for protracted periods. Certainly, the installation of watering systems on many courses has helped overall, but these cannot negate the problems caused by climatic extremes, and the question of when, and how much, to water remains a major problem for Clerks of the Course. Also, in some cases, attempts at improvement – especially of drainage – have created new problems.

Inappropriate systems, creating 'patchy' going, do not help the race-horse, who needs identical conditions under all four feet to maintain balance. Furthermore, systems which produce different conditions on different sides of the track (or which do not redress existing natural features which create this) can cause the starting 'draw' to have a predominant influence on the outcome of races.

Another problem is that water is often (necessarily) obtained from ponds located on the racecourse, and this is likely to be unfiltered and contaminated with fine particles. These may be responsible for the amount of dust now rising from many courses during dry weather and they may also, over time, compromise the efficiency of the drainage system. A practical way to minimize the amount of fines introduced from ponds is to extract water from the top layer and periodically remove sediment from the bottom.

Racing has also been a traditional sport in countries with hot climates – such as the Arab States – where there is a lack of turf and much of the racing has traditionally taken place on sand surfaces. As racing developed more commercially in the USA, that country also moved towards sand or 'dirt' based tracks, influenced not only by the problems associated with turf maintenance in climatic extremes, but also by the tendency to use tracks not only for extensive periods of racing, but also as permanent training bases, with large numbers of horses working daily on the course itself.

This arrangement, which pertains currently, has proved far from ideal. Perhaps exacerbated by the tightness of many courses, the surfaces used are associated with a high incidence of physical problems and, in many States, the racing authorities permit horses to run on medication (for lameness/pain relief and pulmonary haemorrhage) which is not permitted in Europe.

Reverting to Britain, the racing authorities decided in the early 1980s that, while the main aim must be to preserve good turf on as many courses as possible, there was also a need to explore artificial surfaces as a means of providing continuity of sport. At that time, wood fibre was being used as a surface for training gallops, but experience elsewhere had indicated that this was not suitable for actual racing. However, the sponsored installation of a gallop at Newmarket, using sand bound together with an oil-based polymer, raised hopes that an all-weather racing surface was achievable. In the light of this, a Jockey Club evaluation team instigated trials at Newmarket of this and an alternative system, the latter being sand bonded together with mono-filament fibre.

Representatives of the racing world were invited to inspect these facilities, and trials, which included jumping some hurdles, were carried out on both surfaces. Conditions at the time were cold and wet, but not freezing. Both surfaces stood up adequately to the passage of several horses at racing pace, but there was evidence of 'kick-back' (surface material flying back at high level) that might affect horses in an actual race.

At a post-trial conference an American consultant, reporting on US experience, was asked: 'If you know how to do it, why don't we copy you?' His reply was that the American record on breakdown of horses was poor, and the hope was that a better system could be found else-where, which America could copy.

Of the two surfaces tested, there was a marginal preference for the fibre-bonded sand, but concern was expressed by some trainers that neither surface would prove suitable for jump racing.

The outcome of the trials was that two racecourses, Lingfield and Southwell, were given approval to install all-weather tracks, each using one of the surfaces demonstrated. Subsequently, a third all-weather track was installed at Wolverhampton.

With appropriate maintenance procedures, both surfaces have proved viable for racing, but there are some drawbacks. Both have demonstrated kick-back problems, and a short-lived excursion into jump racing was abandoned by the authorities when drawbacks became apparent. It is noteworthy that many horses show different form on all-weather surfaces as compared to turf, and relatively few campaign successfully (indeed, at all) on both surfaces. It may also be significant that very few British trainers run their better horses on the all-weather tracks, and the general class of all-weather runners is moderate.

Subsequent to the trials on the two all-weather surfaces, an experi-mental gallop was devised and installed, using a grit sand and rubber mix. This worked well in tests, produced minimal kick-back, and was frostproof. Although the British Jockey Club declined to pursue this, it was demonstrated to a committee appointed by the Swedish racing authorities, who were seeking a replacement for the wood fibre surface at Malmo racecourse.

After further trials and evaluation, the Swedish committee selected this surface, and a specification as close as possible to the experimental gallop was agreed. Although the rubber material could be supplied from the UK, the base material and sand were to be sourced locally to Malmo, the racecourse authorities being responsible for construction.

For some months after construction the new course rode well, but during summer it became necessary to water. Within a short time kick-back had increased, and the horses came in very dirty. Upon investigation, samples obtained indicated that a very fine, clay-bearing sand had been used in construction of the course. Furthermore, the water supply came from the bottom layers of a disused gravel pit, and this may have contributed clay washings left after gravel extraction. This experience confirmed once again that the selection of sand is a crucial factor in constructing all-weather surfaces, and that any surface will fail eventually if fines and other contamination build up beyond a certain level.

Future Possibilities

The ideal surface for racehorses is natural turf growing in shallow, free-draining topsoil on solid chalk. The qualities of this surface are that it is resilient, supporting but not jarring the horse; it allows some degree of penetration, providing the grip and purchase necessary for a full speed, balanced gallop, and it permits controlled deceleration – an important factor in avoiding leg injuries when 'pulling up' or when a horse has to be 'snatched up' during a race.

Since none of the all-weather surfaces currently available fully replicate these qualities, they can be considered only a partial success. However, recent research suggests that there may be a way forward. Innovative uses of a fibred rubber (detailed in Chapter 19) have proved very successful in both reinforcing turf and replicating its qualities in a variety of contexts, equestrian and otherwise. If these qualities can be incorporated into racing surfaces, the potential exists for radical advances. The main areas being explored are as follows.

Turf reinforcement

It has already been demonstrated that, a relatively low cost, it is possible to reinforce existing turf and to improve availability in adverse weather conditions. This is now proven in areas such as dressage arenas, polo lawns and major showgrounds. While there is still a need for periods of rest and regeneration between uses, these are significantly reduced in comparison to untreated natural turf. In this context, the system might permit more frequent use of existing turf racecourses, with less wear.

Protection of turf and horses

In the field of eventing, it has already proved possible to top-dress areas of turf with this material to provide a temporary safe surface on what would otherwise be poached, frosty or damaged ground. After use, the material can either be recovered, or left to be absorbed into the turf to minimize further damage. On a turf racecourse, this use has obvious

Reinforced turf showing resistance to poaching, despite heavy use in wet weather.

potential, one area of special interest being the take-off and landing areas on jumping courses. In the interests of safety, it might be useful to extend treatment of the landing side of fences to cover the 'fall' area which, at racing pace, can extend well beyond where a horse would normally be expected to land.

Divot replacement

At present, racecourses replace those divots that cannot be 'trodden in' with fine sand. Filling with the fibre/grit sand mixture could augment the measures described above, and have a beneficial effect on resistance to poaching, grass regeneration, and drainage.

Obviously, full testing of these proposals, using methods simulating racecourse conditions, would be necessary before they could be employed in actual course preparation and maintenance. The turf reinforcement and ground protection functions could, initially, be tested on training gallops and, if the jumping option were to be explored, on various schooling grounds. Regarding divot replacement, it would be a simple matter to carry out controlled experiments to establish the optimum fibre/sand mix and subsequent rate of top dressing required. Current research, related to polo lawns, is examining the benefits off adding one-third by volume of *Springway Fibre* (see Chapter 19) to a divot-filling medium.

Provided that such tests proved satisfactory, it might, by using a combination of the techniques described, prove possible to preserve the essential nature of British racing on natural turf courses, and to keep meetings – including jumping fixtures – flowing under most weather conditions.

If the surface provided proved very successful and hard-wearing it might, in the future, be possible for racecourses to improve their financial situation by broadening the track area in front of the stands and making this, and the racecourse facilities, available for major showjumping and dressage competitions.

17.

Indoor Surfaces

COVERING AN ARTIFICIAL surface with a building eliminates two problems, the potential for the surface to blow away, and the risk of freezing. It does, however, become essential to water for dust control and, if the selected material requires it, to lock the surface together. The fact that you need to water means that a drainage system is required to cope with overwatering, although the volume of run-off will be limited. (With reference to this, we have recently installed a *Springway Conduit Base System*, as described in Chapter 7, to provide moisture control for an indoor school.) The installation of an overhead spray system is possible because the structure is there to support it. It is also worth considering storing rainwater collected from the roof to ensure availability and minimize cost.

Generally, an indoor arena has to justify its cost by multi--discipline use. The width is normally limited by cost and structural considerations. These two factors mean that the surface must be capable of permitting turning at speed, without breakaway occurring.

Since the surface is protected from wind, you can consider using lightweight wood-based products such as wood shavings. Peat has also been used. Both peat and shavings are usually blended with sand. However, since the surface has to be kept wet, rot can still be a problem.

Even with an indoor arena, the surface will still break down to fines, and you can keep on topping up with large but short-life material. A situation will then arise where the surface is very deep, the perimeter structure will be supporting surplus material, the doors will not open

Portable arena for the J.A. Allen-sponsored dressage display, BETA 1997 – Equitred fibre on a matting base.

and the surface is unsafe. At this point you have to dig the lot out and start again. Therefore, a long-life material may be more economical over a period.

Since it is essential to minimize material breakdown and avoid dirt being brought into the arena, it is desirable to have a warm-up area or collecting ring off the main arena. This should have a surface similar to the main arena and, to a degree, will act as a sacrificial area to minimize the amount of mud, etc. carried into the main arena. Maintenance equipment, jumps etc. should be stored in a similar protected area.

With an indoor arena, it is not essential for the base to be frostproof. This means that relatively low-cost materials can be used for the base. Correctly laid chalk as a base, with an appropriate surface, may be a good choice.

Maintenance will generally be identical to that of a similar surface outdoors; dragging, harrowing or rotovating. It is necessary to keep any perimeter boards clear of surface material and to ensure that doors are free to open.

A very specialized area is the provision of temporary indoor surfaces. Here, certain major shows have developed their own techniques for re-using a batch of material, often soil-based, which has been carefully stored between shows. Over the last few years, we ourselves have provided a portable arena system for the British Equestrian Trade Association. Improvements have been made to this and it has, for several years, withstood use for dressage displays, confirming that a surface can be provided which will cope with most equestrian activities. However, provision of the requisite surface qualities, especially with regard to safety, requires considerable experience and expertise, and it is unlikely that such systems could be operated by individuals.

It is possible that, in the future, matting-based systems could be used, but development work and trials would be necessary.

18.

Health, Safety and Environmental Issues

IN GENERAL, THE main materials used for arena construction – sand, plastic, rubber and wood – are in common use and should not cause problems. Indeed, recycling plastic and rubber for this purpose must be more environmentally friendly than alternative disposal by landfill or incineration.

Waste Rubber from Tyres

With many artificial surfaces now incorporating recycled material from tyres, this use has become a major disposal route for tyre waste. For safety reasons, however, it is essential that such waste is wire-free. Since, for some years, most car tyres have contained wire reinforcement, this limited the means of recycling and, for a time, availability of suitable tyre material for all-weather surfaces was reduced. However, following environmental problems with toxic gases produced by incineration, legislation introduced in 2003 required the granulation of all tyres and there has recently been considerable investment in granulation plants, which include machinery to extract the wire. Since it is proposed that all disposal to landfill will be banned by 2006, there will presumably be a glut of this material available for the foreseeable future.

While much of the material produced by the new plants is of smaller size than was formerly the case, most of it is safe and suitable for all-weather surfaces. However, there is still available, from some sources, rubber waste recovered from aircraft tyres. Since these do not contain wire, their waste material is potentially safer than that from other sources, and it tends to be of superior quality. It is, however, more expensive. At the time of writing, it is also possible that wire-free car tyres may, once again, be produced by certain manufacturers, which could lead to the future availability of wire-free waste from this source.

Oils and Preservatives

There have been attempts to prolong the life of wood fibre by treating with preservatives, such as creosote. These materials have to be applied using face masks and protective clothing. Inhalation of contaminated wood dust has to be considered a possible hazard.

Dust deriving from other materials associated with all-weather surfaces can also be both a nuisance and a potential hazard. It is generally controlled by bonding the surface with either water or oil-based products, including wax. However, when the latter are used, the efficacy of dust control becomes crucial, because dust contaminated with oil or wax represents an additional hazard to health. Furthermore, materials such as oil will leach into drainage systems, contaminating water courses. The health and environmental risks associated with oil-based materials can be minimized by using materials already tested and approved for other purposes. One major oil company will only supply material for dust suppression which has been approved for agricultural use as a crop spray.

Water Conservation

Water conservation has now become a major factor as demand is exceeding supply. Legislation is making it necessary for installers and operators of sports surfaces to demonstrate by monitoring and treating facilities that any water discharged into drainage systems does not contaminate water supplies.

General Safety

It is worth checking that the installation itself does not create safety hazards. For example, post and rail fencing and kicking boards should be installed well back from the track, to avoid leg contact. Drainage ditches can create risk if the horse spooks and leaves the arena or gallop; a shallow grassed gulley will provide adequate run-off and soakaway at lower cost and reduced hazard. Any drain covers near arenas should have non-slip surfaces and be of adequate strength to support the weight of a horse.

Most artificial surfaces require time and use to consolidate and key to the base. For safety reasons, as well as to improve the arena, a period of careful riding-in is desirable. Start off with flatwork and progress to speed work, fast turns and jumping as you become confident that the surface is safe and will not break away. Note that most surfaces require a minimum depth to avoid this. If you have a membrane with insufficient surface material to protect it, you have a tripping hazard. Equally, if a surface is permitted to ride too deep, or the horse breaks through the surface, damage to the horse, for example a strained back or tendon, is likely.

Finally, fire may be a hazard, especially in an indoor arena which has a combustible surface. Therefore, smoking in the vicinity should never be permitted. Likewise, extreme care is necessary in an indoor school if carrying out any maintenance work requiring blow lamps or welding equipment. As with all things, common sense and care can help avoid accidents.

19.

A New Project: Reinforced Turf

THERE HAVE BEEN various attempts to reinforce turf, some by incorporating plastic mesh or blocks in the soil. These have not always been successful, because frost and growth tend to bring the reinforcement to the surface and it becomes a tripping hazard.

Our first experimental arena base was carved out of chalk. This left a perimeter track around the outside of the arena, about a metre wide, of exposed chalk. The rubber-bonded fibre we laid is very resilient, and some bounced over the surround boards and took some grit sand with it. We noticed that, within a short period, natural regeneration of turf and local plant life was taking place on the perimeter track. This turf was wear-resistant to horses in the field, remained green in dry weather, and was preferentially grazed by the horses.

With hindsight this was not surprising; the fibre had originally been used with the intention of simulating the root structure of turf, and it was a good growing medium. In other locations such as The Severals warm-up track at Newmarket and the Park Arena at Goodwood, the spillover was onto existing turf. At these venues the fibre was absorbed into the turf very quickly. At Goodwood, the fibre-impregnated turf was mown with no problems.

Where arenas are used for dressage, the surrounding turf is used to ride the horse in before entering the arena. The fibre-treated turf was standing up to hard use during competitions with minimum turf damage. At Goodwood, with the permission of the Duke of Richmond, a turf was cut from The Park Arena perimeter, upon which fibre had

A purpose-laid *Springway Fibre* riding-in track around an all-weather arena. This concept was originally inspired by spillover of arena material onto surrounding turf.

been spilling for five years. It was found that over this period, the fibre had been incorporated into the turf to a depth of 50 mm.

The Racecourse Maintenance Superintendent who dug the turf was of the opinion that the nearby National Hunt course, Fontwell, could be improved by similar treatment. Nature seemed to be telling us something!

Early Equestrian Experiments

It is safer to try out new ideas in practice when horses are performing individually and, with the approval of the relevant course builders and stewards, the fibre was laid on sections of horse trials courses to improve going. The first time was at Brockenhurst. The fibre was laid on take-off and landing zones of the last two jumps on the cross-country course the day before a spring competition. The fibre was visible, and 500 horses were ridden over it with no problems. By the time of the autumn competition, the grass had regenerated through the fibre, which was no longer visible. Again, 500 horses used the course: the surface was resilient and suffered minimal damage.

Further testing was subsequently carried out, including laying artificial bases in a manner similar to gallop construction. This was done at warm-up jumps, which take a tremendous pounding, and also ravine and coffin jumps, where the ground suffers more than at a straightforward obstacle.

These tests showed that the fibre can be used as a very long-life reinforcement for turf and also as a growing medium. Over a period of time it is capable of adding resilience to turf, and this is of particular value when equestrian events are held in dry weather conditions, when watering is not possible, or excessively expensive. This suggested particular value to locations used for major events two or three times a year, especially if jumping is part of the programme. However, some locations also hold dressage competitions on grass several times a year. This can put a considerable stress on the area of grass used. It occurred to us that it would be beneficial for such venues to treat a suitable area so that the precise location of arenas could be varied.

A cross-country practice fence at Brockenhurst, sited on an 'above ground' all-weather surface.

Lucinda Green taking one of the jumps with an all-weather landing area at Rademon; another such jump is in the background.

All-weather take-off and landing areas at a fence in the Irish National Championships, Rademon.

Also, it seemed possible that private owners with limited resources might treat an area of grass as a low-cost alternative to laying an all-weather arena. With sensible use it seemed that this would at least provide good going during periods of very dry weather.

Other Experiments and Uses

Another possible use for this type of treatment which occurred to us was that it could help resolve the problem where overuse of bridleways and pathways is preventing natural regeneration. We felt that our equestrian experiments had perhaps identified a new aspect of turf management; that there were many situations, other than equestrian, where reinforced turf would be of value. As frequent visitors to the Royal Horticultural Gardens at Wisley, and to various National Trust properties, we were aware of the amount of unintentional damage done to turf by visitors and their cars.

A local nursery offered to experiment in their display gardens. They decided to dig out the damaged area, incorporate fibre plus grit sand and reseed. The Curator and Grass Specialist from Wisley examined turf where fibre had been absorbed. They considered it worthwhile conducting trials of their own. They selected a trial area where the turf had been completely destroyed by overuse, and ground compaction was damaging an adjacent specimen tree. They cultivated the area, incorporating fibre in the soil, and returfed.

Poached ground after dressing with *Springway Fibre*/sand mix.

Regenerated grass.

It was discovered that an alternative treatment is to top-dress with the fibre. In the growing season the turf will grow into and absorb the fibre very quickly. Further dressings can be applied as necessary to build up the degree of resilience and protection required in high-stress areas. In low spots with poor drainage, a coarse grit sand can be added as an additional dressing. Grass seed can be added to bare patches and will germinate and grow on. Mowing is no problem, although it may be helpful to leave the grass a little longer than normal until regeneration is complete. The fibred rubber also provides some measure of frost protection owing to improved drainage and thermal insulation.

In 1993, several National Trust properties began carrying out trials to see whether such treatment would help preserve turf in their gardens. Proposals were also considered regarding problems arising in some National Parks – the Peak District, and the New Forest, for example. The car is making it possible for many people to visit such areas but, unfortunately, by doing so in great numbers, they risk destroying the very thing they come to see. Therefore, the possibility of providing additional, reinforced, paths and bridleways was examined.

Further experiments were carried out by the Department of Environmental Biology at Manchester University. Their studies confirmed that, when the fibre is added to turf, the critical root structure of the turf is increased. They also found that, when tested for ball bounce and roll, the treated turf had more consistent properties than untreated areas. This improvement, achieved in part by incorporating stone-sized pieces

Turf growing through *Springway Fibre*.

A *Springway Fibre* gallop.

of material, may have implications for a whole range of sports – at the time of writing, we are in consultation with a major polo club, as explained in Chapter 20.

The Position at Present

Since the second edition of this book was published, reinforced turf has proved its worth. The system has become accepted by The Institute of Groundsmanship and the Sports Turf Research Institute and we have patented it as *Springway Fibre*. Installations of reinforced turf are proving of value in the following situations:

On lawns around National Trust properties, and a chateau in France.

On footpaths and cliff top areas.

In dressage arenas.

On cross-country courses and gallops (these uses have indicated the potential for improving racecourse surfaces, as described in Chapter 16).

Shows often have to cope with poor weather conditions.

Reinforced turf withstands the passage of Shire horses and drays at the Highland Show.

At major shows where, under poor weather conditions, it has confirmed that it can be a low-cost method of providing better going.

A major university in America has adopted the system for use on their sports surfaces.

As work continues on this project, it will be fascinating to see what other uses lie ahead. Any improvements to natural surfaces for equestrian and other uses must be welcome, especially if they can be made in an environmentally friendly way, safely recycling large quantities of otherwise waste material.

20.

The Way Forward – a Future for Equestrian Sport

T HE EQUESTRIAN WORLD is divided into many individual disciplines and, at present, it seems that the governing bodies of each believe that they can continue to survive as entirely separate activities. The reality, however, is that most equestrian sports are facing organizational and financial difficulties. This lack of organization – and inter-disciplinary co-operation – has, among other issues, led to a dearth of venues suitable for major events, as evidenced by the lack of a suitable location for a 50th Royal Anniversary pageant.

This situation contrasts rather oddly with the fact that most race-courses, and those stadiums that do exist, are used for only a few days each year. Surely, given the advances in the development of artificial surfaces and improved construction methods for stadiums it should, with proper co-operation, be possible to rectify the shortfall of facilities in a manner beneficial to all equestrian sports.

We would like to conclude this book by summarizing the current situation for the various equestrian sports, and giving our opinion of how new technology and greater co-operation could be of benefit to all.

Racing

At present, some of the best going is found on certain point-to-point courses, which are preserved by traditional methods and which have the advantage of limited use, free from the economic pressures which such use imposes on commercial courses. An example of this was the opening meeting of the 1999 point-to-point season at Larkhill. A large number of horses raced on very good going in front of a big crowd, on a day when all National Hunt meetings south of Newcastle (official going: 'heavy') had been abandoned. A glance at the *Horse and Hound* point-to-point chart highlights the reason – approximately 100 different sites, mainly farmland, host between them approximately 150 meetings: the grass has time to regenerate.

We feel that it is important to preserve purely natural turf on some of the major historic courses – Newmarket, Epsom, Cheltenham and Aintree, for example – and that the economic consequences of limited use could be offset by increased use of the stands, and the provision of facilities for other equestrian events, as discussed in Chapter 16. For many other courses, however, use of the turf reinforcement system

A traditional point-to-point course (Larkhill) providing good going in wet weather.

could provide the key to greater availability and to better, safer, racing conditions in times of inclement weather.

So far as completely artificial surfaces are concerned, it does seem possible to provide systems with minimal kick-back and reduced maintenance requirements. If the will existed, it would be possible to resurface at least one of the existing all-weather tracks with a more modern system which might (subject to testing) prove suitable for jump racing.

Eventing

Ground used for eventing has to cope with very intensive use once or twice a year, often in poor weather conditions. The use of turf reinforcement has already proved valuable in certain parts of courses subjected to high stress, serving both to protect the ground and improve safety. Given the success of the reinforced warm-up area at Burghley, it is to be hoped that such uses will be expanded to include the dressage and showjumping arenas and, possibly, the steeplechase section. The

Practice arena at Burghley: a *Springway* reinforced turf surface (inset: the track after four days use).

material is now available in sufficient quantity and at a cost that would make this viable.

Other Disciplines

Surfaces, whether artificial or reinforced turf, are now available to suit any equestrian activity. For example, arena polo, a new and growing version of the sport, is making use of some very successful wax-bound surfaces.

Shortly before drafting this new edition, we began consultation with the Guards Polo Club with reference to full-size polo lawns. At the time of writing, we are conducting trials on an existing lawn area with the *Springway Fibre* turf reinforcement system, with additional top dressing being applied as the fibre is absorbed into the turf. We are also adding one-third by volume of the fibre to the divot filling medium. It is hoped

Arena polo on a Eurotrack wax-bound surface.

that these trials will demonstrate that applications of *Springway Fibre* will allow increased use of existing lawns at very low cost.

The possibility of installing a full-size artificial polo surface incorporating a *Springway Conduit Base System* for drainage has also been mooted. Since a polo lawn is so large (normally 275 x 180 m), this would inevitably involve considerable costs and would not proceed without appropriate installation trials. However, we now have a system developed which could, in principle, cope with the drainage of such a large area and the inquiry itself is indicative of the way in which some sports are embracing the innovations in artificial surfaces. As mentioned earlier, it is our view that, if major projects of this nature are to take shape in the future, the cost of providing and maintaining new facilities could best be met by co-operation and sharing.

Springway Fibre being sprayed over the Guards' polo ground, Smith's Lawn, Windsor. Small dressings were added incrementally to build up the required going which would enhance ball roll.

Smith's Lawn after spraying with *Springway Fibre*.

The Royal Enclosure at Smith's Lawn after turf reinforcement and reseeding.

Polo action on the reinforced surface at Smith's Lawn.

County Shows

In addition to their equestrian content, county shows often have classes for other livestock, and they are attended by a wide variety of heavy vehicles in addition to the spectators' cars. This all adds up to heavy use of what is often private land, which has to be returned to the owners after the show in a condition that will persuade them that it is worth loaning/leasing again in subsequent years. In most cases, it is neither feasible nor financially viable for such venues to lay artificial arenas, so this is a case where turf reinforcement can provide some protection at low cost, as has been demonstrated at the Highland Show.

In adverse weather conditions, reinforcement of approach tracks and parking areas could be especially valuable in reducing damage, with the material being either left in place after the show to encourage grass regeneration, or recovered for future use.

It seems to us that a way forward exists. It is up to the governing bodies, such as the British Horse Society and the British Horseracing Board, to explore these ideas in more detail, hopefully in a spirit of co-operation, so that equestrian sport in all forms can develop and thrive.

Index

Note: Page numbers in **bold** refer to
illustrations

additives, oil/wax 65, 67–9
affordability 71–2
arenas
    access track 57, 72
    alternatives to 72
    amount and type of use 70
    dressage 42–8, 52, **53**, **62**, 92–3
    failure of 58–9
    selection of features 70–1
    showjumping **62**, 66
    site selection 29–30
    temporary/portable 87, 88
asphalt base 40–1, 68

base 17, 25–6, 72
    area of 38
    below ground level **38**, 39
    break-up of 40, 49
    drainage 39–40, 59
    experimental system 42–8
    gallops 76, 78
    indoor arena 87
    lunge arena 74–5
    Springway Conduit System 13, 35,
        39–40, 44
base materials 40
    asphalt 40–1, **68**
    chalk 21, 40
    concrete 42–4
boards, perimeter 57, 87–8
bonded surfaces 67–9, 78, 79, 82
    maintenance 54
    monofilament fibres 54, 67, 78, 82
    oils/waxes 67–9, 90
British Equestrian Trade Association
    (BETA) 19, **87**, 88
British Standards, concrete and building
    sand 36
Brockenhurst horse trials 93–4

Burghley horse trials 103

Carluke **62**
chalk 21, 40
clay materials, in sands/grits 51
concrete 42–4
concrete sand 36
conduit system 42–8
contamination of surfaces 49–50, 57, 72
contractor 27–8, 41, 71, 73
    maintenance of surface 28
    site selection 30
costs
    affordability 71–2
    base 60
    capital 26
    maintenance 26, 71
county shows 107–8
covered school, *see* indoor school
cross-country courses 84–5, 93–4, **95**
cushioning 21

'dirt' race tracks 81, 82
divot replacement 85
dragging of surfaces 66
drain covers 91
drainage 25–6, 39–41
    across-the-base system 59
    combined with watering system 78–9
    conduit system 42–8
    failure 51, 59
    slope 15
    surface materials 35
    under-base system 39–40
drainage ditches 91
dressage arena **62**
    construction 42–8
    maintenance 52, **53**
    ride-in track 44, **48**, 92–3
dust 58
dust control
    indoor arena 86

oil/wax-bound surfaces 67, 90
see also watering

Easterton Farm, Perth **56**
electric cable sheathing 33, 65
elephant pump 42, **46**
environmental issues 12, 89–90
Equitred fibre **87**
Essen Equitana 18
Eurotrack surface **68**
evaporation, from surface 41
eventing 84–5, 103–4

failure of surfaces 51, 58–9
  causes 58
  oil-bound 67, 69
fences, cross-country 93–4, **95**
fencing 90–1
fibre-bonded sand 54, 67, 78, 82
fibred rubber 16, **17**, 33, **34**, **65**
  costs 61
  gallops **77**
  maintenance 53, 54
fibred rubber/sand surface 59, 61, 65–6,
  82–3
fines 49–51, 67, 69
fire hazards 91
Fontwell racecourse 93
freezing-thawing, base materials 40

gallops 23
  base construction 76, 78
  maintenance 78–9
  reinforced turf **98**
  site selection 29–30
  surface materials 76, **77**
  warm-up tracks 29, **30**, 76
  width 76
gardens, turf reinforcement 96–7
Goodwood 18, 92–3
grass, *see* turf
Green, Lucinda **95**
grit sand/fibred rubber surface 59, 61,
  65–6, 82–3
grits 31, **32**
guarantees 28, 71
Guards Polo Club 104–5, **106–7**

harrowing of surfaces 55
Highland Show **100**
horse
  effects of surfaces on performance and
    soundness 82, 83
  impact on surfaces 21

Horse Guards Parade **68**
horse trials 93–5, 103–4

ideal surface
  general riding 21
  racehorses 83
indoor arenas/surfaces 23, 41, 86–8
  fire hazard 91
  maintenance 87–8
  materials 86–7
  warm-up area 87
installation
  evaluation 60
  responsibility for 27–8, 72
  safety 90–1
  timing 72
Institute of Groundsmanship 99

jar test 49–50, 59
Jockey Club 82–3
jump racing 82

kick-back **77**, 78, 82, 83
kicking boards 90–1

Larkill point-to-point course 102
levelling, equipment 55, **56**
lifespan of surfaces 70
liner, *see* membrane
Lingfield racecourse 82
local materials 13, 26
lunge arena
  construction of 74–5
  size 75
  uses and value of 72, 74
lungeing 52

maintenance 52–4
  bonded surfaces 54
  contract 28
  costs 26, 71
  equipment 55–7
  indoor arenas 87–8
  lunge arena 75
  schedule 54
  and use of surface 52
  wood surfaces 64
Manchester University, Department of
  Environmental Biology 97
March, Lord 18
materials
  migration 49–51
  recycled 12–13, 26, 33, **34**
  sourcing 13, 26, 27

see also base materials; surface
    materials
membrane 23, 26, 40
mica 51
monofilament fibres 51
monofilament-bonded sand 54, 67,
    78, 82

National Parks 97
National Trust properties 97
Newmarket
    The Severals warm-up track **30**, 67,
        78, 92
    trials of all-weather gallops 81

oil-based additives 65, 90
oil-bound surfaces 67–9
Olympic Games 18

Park Arena, Goodwood 92–3
peat 86
perimeter boards 57, 87–8
plastic wastes 15, 16, 33, 64–5
    costs 61
    sourcing 36–7
point-to-point courses 101–2
polo
    all-weather arena 104
    reinforcement of turf lawns 85, 104–5,
        106–7
ponds, as water supply 44, **47**, 57, 81
portable arena **87**, 88
preservatives, wood 90
problems
    with operation 73
    with surface construction 24
    see also failure
project responsibility 27–8, 41, 71
    use of contractor 27–8
PVC granules 33, 61, 65

quarry-based materials 12, 13, 36

racecourses 79
    divot replacement 85
    drawbacks to artificial surfaces 82
    maintenance 52
    point-to-point 101–2
    sand/'dirt' (US) 81, 82
    turf reinforcement 102–3
    use of facilities 85
racing 101–3
    jump 82, 103
Rademon horse trials **95**

recycled materials 12–13, 26, 33, **34**
reinforced turf, *see* turf reinforcement
Richmond, Duke of 92
riding-in, of surfaces 72, 91
riding-in track 92–3
road construction, membrane 23, 26
roadstone 40, 44
roller **56**
rolling 53, 57
rotovation 54, 55, 57
rubber materials 33, **34**, 64–6, 89–90
    availability and sourcing 12–13, 36–7
    see also fibred rubber

safety issues 90–1
Sale of Good Act 35
sand 31, **32**, 63
    adding plastic and rubber materials
        58, 64
    costs 61
    fibre-bonded 54, 67, 78, 82
    grades 36, 63
    jar test 50, 59
    kick-back 78
    maintenance of surfaces 63
    monofilament-bonded 54, 67, 78, 82
    in premixed materials 37
    sourcing 35–6
    washing 36, 61
    washing *in situ* 59
The Severals warm-up track, Newmarket
    30, 67, **78**, 92
show grounds **99**, 100, 107–8
show jumping arenas **62**, 66
silica sand 31
site 24–5
    levelling 39
    selection of 29–30, 71
    sloping 39
    waterlogged 39–40
size of arena 25
Smith's Lawn **106**, **107**
Southwell racecourse 82
Sports Turf Research Institute 99
Springway Conduit Base System 13, 35,
    39–40, 44, 86, 105
Springway Fibre turf 13–14, 44, **48**, 85,
    98, 99
    present installations 99–100
stones, rising to surface 40, 49
surface materials 25
    addition of plastic/rubber materials
        58, 64
    clean up of 58–9, 67

contamination 49–50, 57, 72
costs 25, 37, 61
cushioning effect 21
depth 25, 54, 63, 91
drainage properties 35
environmental issues 89–90
evaporation 41
fines build-up 49–51, 67, 69
gallops 76, **77**
indoor arena 86–7
jar test 49–50, 59
kick-back **77**, 78, 82, 83
lunge arena 75
maintenance 54
maintenance equipment 55–7
obtaining samples 35
oil or wax bound 67–9, 79
plastic wastes 33, 64–5
premixing 37, **43**
remixing 55, 57
replacement 58
riding-in/consolidation 72, 91
rubber-based 33, **34**, 64–6
sand 31, **32**, 63
sourcing 35–7
topping up/replacing 54
watering 41–2
wood wastes 31–3, 61, 64, 76, 90
Sweden 83

temporary surfaces, indoor **87**, 88
transportation costs 35, 37, 61
turf
    drawbacks of 22, 80–1
    on point-to-point courses 101–2
    qualities as riding surface 21, 83
turf reinforcement 72, 83–5, 92–100
    dressage ride-in track 44, **48**
    early equestrian experiments 93–6
    horse trials 93–5, 103–4
    non-equestrian uses 96–9

polo grounds 85, 104–5, **106–7**
present installations 99–100
racecourses 102–3
show grounds 107–8
turf growth through **98**
tyre wastes 12–13, 33, **34**, 65–6, 89–90
    costs 61
    sourcing 36–7

United States, all-weather race tracks
    81, 82
use of surfaces, amount and type 70

Village Farm arena **17**

warm-up arena 103
warm-up tracks, gallops 29, **30**, 76
water conservation 12, 41–2, 90
water run-off 41
water supply 41–2, 44, 57, 81
watering
    combined with drainage system 78–9
    equipment 57
    fibred rubber/grit sand surface 66
    gallops 78–9
    sand surfaces 63
    turf racetracks 80, 81
    under-surface 57
waterlogged sites 39–40
wax additives 65, 90
wax-bound surfaces 67–9, 79
Wisley Royal Horticultural Gardens 96
Wolverhampton racecourse 82
wood fibre 31–3, 76
    costs 61
    lifespan 70
    maintenance 64
    safety issues 90
    sourcing 35
wood shavings 86